An Awakening

Clear Passage Through Life's Storms

Personal and practical insights, tips and techniques to help you move through challenging times.

An Awakening

Clear Passage Through Life's Storms

This is a work of nonfiction and any names, dates and stories have been kept anonymous to protect their privacy.

TABLE OF CONTENTS

MY STORY

I've been a student of life most of my life—a student who measures success not only by college degrees but by a passion for learning and a drive to share what I learn. For much of my life I traveled the world, crafted innovative business models, cared for sick people, encouraged elders/families through challenging times, helped people expand ideas, wrote/played music, and wrote/produced many types of publications from books to scripts to videos. For most of my life, these activities brought me joy.

Five years ago I experienced a major life transition—the passion for my work died and I couldn't get it back. So I stepped back from a successful career and stepped into uncertainty. During this time I lived off past fruits of my labors and regrouped. Just as I was about to reenter a new life, a sickness knocked me down and then it hit the world.

COVID-19 got me in late 2019 and I became quite ill. For six weeks I could barely function and then developed a *long COVID syndrome* for the next eighteen months. When I recovered to some degree and began working from home, I refocused on my writing skills as a way to educate people about realities of the pandemic and to support professionals who tried to care for them.

However, growing amounts of misinformation, driven by perverse political incentives, began skewing facts and sucking in multiple victims. This misinformation grew into legions of *disinformation campaigns* where people ignored experts who actually knew what to do; then the clowns and fools stepped up and people who actually listened to them paid a high price.

Some of us lost loved ones, some of us lost our health, some of us recovered and some of us continue to deny the pandemic ever existed. As time passed everyone suffered and many of us realized that one day we will each take our last breath and end our earthly existence. Many of us examined our own life purpose, let go of "stuff" that had little meaning anymore, and moved forward with a bit more determination.

My Awakening

My own spiritual awakening began in my thirties as my life collapsed. My marriage ended, I had to relocate, my mother developed Alzheimer's disease, my father nearly died from a medical problem, my best friend died of breast cancer, my nephew was born on life support, and a career I loved abruptly ended. I learned during challenging times in life, you either overcome them or they overtake you. It was here I began a journey inward. For so many people around the world, the pandemic's impact led them on a similar journey of inner awakening and greater awareness.

Living on Purpose

I began writing this book during my recovery from COVID and it took me two years to complete it. During this time, I reframed my own vision around growing older, regained my health, relaunched my musical interests, rebranded my business and revived an online presence.

It was also a time to rebalance relationships. Certain people who had been in my life for years drifted away; I jettisoned other negative people, and aligned with more enlightened individuals.

Learning to Fly

It's important to know the pandemic did not cause the problems we experienced; it exposed existing problems. Before the pandemic began, I'd grown weary of climbing *Mount Greed* and had walked away from the swamps and cattle drives of healthcare and aging services. All of it had become a life sucking, soul draining way of life and I had to move on.

In learning to fly, I let go of toxic situations that wore me down and found an inner light to lift me up. Sometimes you have to tear it all down to rebuild something whole—something whole that brings a coherence and calmness to your life.

Finding My Voice

Meditation practices became a ritual that began and ended each day; I spent time writing and producing tutorials and educational materials. I renewed a passion for learning and surrounded myself with positive people who share my values with a focus on health and life balance.

I learned when insurmountable problems threaten personal survival, you either become extinct or rise above the limitations and evolve. It's never too late to start over.

INTRODUCTION

As civilizations emerge from bunkers to a changed world, much of life seems the same. However, we've been propelled into a new future—a future where institutions (government, education, healthcare, finance, and even family/tribe) are forever altered.

Life's Perfect Storms

The global pandemic, and the economic crises it's caused, led to rapid deployments of at-home workforces, virtual networking, telehealth visits, remote learning, and multiple business closures; in short, chaos. Novel words embedded into our lexicon such as curb-side pickup, social distancing, masking, ubiquitous access, covidiot, contactless delivery, self-isolation—the list goes on and on. So what happened and where are we now?

First, A Worldwide Disruption

The pandemic is referred to as a "Black Swan" event—an event that is unpredictable, unforeseen, and one with extreme consequences. But was it unforeseen or was it actually an event predicted for decades? Were warnings ignored and then denied?

The Coronavirus, a contagious killer virus, led to Covid disease and then to coverups. **Yes,** this type of event had been predicted for years and was ignored for months when it first began.

The United States (US) reacted medically but had no overall plan or unified approach. A weakened Center for Disease Control (CDC), a vacuum of leadership, no sense of accountability, states all doing their own thing, and inconsistent messaging led our country to be number one in sickness, in deaths, and in anger.

Diseases know no politics and when all else failed leaders ignored the facts and focused on magical thinking. Pretending it will go away is never a strategy. It was an anxious and frightening time for people as every aspect of daily life defaulted.

We bore witness to how dependent hospitals were for the revenue of elective procedures; how senior congregate living settings became killing fields and exposed the long known issues of poor staffing and lack of infection control practices. We learned how dependent so much of society is on school systems for social programs such as childcare and nutrition.

Society splintered showing how little we valued the most vulnerable around us allowing them to be devoured in the name of personal rights. We went from fighting the pandemic to fighting each other.

Second, The Rise of Disinformation

Clarity and consistency became additional casualties as online *opinions* morphed into *believed facts*. People lined up and followed people who spoke loudly but knew little, and drew facts from the opinions of others who deliberately pushed disinformation and conspiracy theories.

What we needed was to inoculate people against fake information put out by fake governments and invalid media sources.

While the pandemic caused painful medical and health challenges, we came face-to-face with unwelcome societal values—values driven by greed and self-interest instead of community.

Third, Our Own Discoveries

Press pause and reflect. Over the past few years so many of us looked at our own lives and began to realize they don't work. Our worlds broke open and we witnessed a lack of health in our healthcare systems, a lack of learning in our education systems, a lack of leadership in governments and a lack of awareness in ourselves.

A paradox for our times is we have more knowledge but less wisdom, more experts but fewer solutions, more guided missiles but misguided thinking. The reality is we cannot solve problems with same thinking, so we stand in a doorway of different choices. What will those choices be for you?

Clear Passage, An Awakening

We've entered a different world and a new normalcy, or at least a new way in which we live our lives.

For the past fifty years, I have been journaling, writing, capturing lessons and gaining insights from my own life as well as from other people along my path. I wrote this book to share with you *eighty-four insights* we all share—some of them we learn early in life, some later and some may be new to you. Some of them will speak to you while others may not matter.

How the Book is Organized

This book divides into four sections that capture the *four forces* of an awakened life: aligning, filtering, connecting and engaging. Spread through the four sections are twelve chapters listing *twelve powers* we experience in life. Each chapter lists seven insights.

Each section can be read consecutively and each chapter can stand alone. Throughout the book there are questions to consider as well as short exercises to help you to go deeper.

The first section (force) examines Alignment. Self-aligning is looking inside yourself, turning in, and knowing who you are. The question examined, "how well do I know myself?"

The second section (force) examines how you sharpen your Filters. Filters uncover how porous you may be, and how you select information aligned with personal beliefs and values. The question asked, "what do I leave in and what do I leave out?"

The third section (force) reveals Connections in various situations. Connections include a Higher Power, inner circles and communities. The question revealed, "who influences me and how do I choose my connections?"

The fourth section (force) explores how you Engage in your own life. Engagement includes elements of personal motivations and interactions with the world in general. The question explored, "what lights me up and how do I stay involved in my own life?"

The closing section lists the eighty-four insights by chapter.

FORCE NUMBER ONE—ALIGNMENT

Alignment is the *first force* when you look into who you are and what is important to you. It responds to the question, "how well do I know myself?"

When your soul and lifeforce align, they flow together and polish your life. This first force examines spiritual alignment which is not just a state of being or a state of mind, but a byproduct of deliberate and purposeful efforts you practice daily. When you align with energies of the Universe, you create a magic and synchronicity in your world.

When you are out of alignment with your higher self, you feel it—you feel it in ways you relate to people, places, and things in your environment. If you feel anything other than joy, you are out of alignment. Your emotional responses function as a barometer of your current alignment. That gut feeling is an intuitive superpower—one where you detect and understand things you cannot explain but can relate to on a spiritual level without a need for conscious reasoning.

This section includes *Chapters One through Three* which focus on the *powers* behind thoughts, beliefs and character as they relate to your own alignment. These three chapters cross *twenty-one insights* to help you calibrate to your own North Star!

CHAPTER ONE—POWER OF THOUGHTS

From your first breath your thoughts formed your experiences and your experiences became your life. Some thoughts consciously changed; others unconsciously repeated. Throughout these times you revealed the person most important to you—yourself.

How you think determines experiences you attract in life, and how you feel is a guide to your current thought patterns. So how do you get to know you? It may seem like a crazy question, but it is one each of us asks ourselves throughout life and definitely at the end of it.

Insight One, Dominant Thoughts

Are you aware of your dominant thoughts? Where do your thoughts spend most of the day? Do you know? What are you tuned into and turned onto? Is your mind a house of constant chatter with moments of clarity or is it pretty clear most of the time? Realize before anything manifests in your life, it first appears as a thought or image in your mind—thoughts and images that are often unconscious. The life you live today reflects past thoughts, and your future unfolds from thoughts you think today.

Your mind is your most powerful tool for creation. You are a living magnet attracting to yourself exactly what you think about. You are literally "what you think," and your character springs from the sum of your thoughts. What do you think about when you think of money? What do you think about when you think of health? What do you think about when you think of family?

Dominate thoughts spring from well-worn programs or paths your mind naturally takes. Think of your subconscious mind as the computer of your life. Is it time to reprogram old files or invest in an upgrade?

Take a few minutes to explore thoughts you are thinking now and write them down. It may seem difficult at first but it gets easier. Think about the "why" behind your focus on unwanted thoughts and how to change them!

For most of my life, my thoughts naturally drifted toward "waiting for the other shoe to drop." From childhood onward if anything went well, I thought it was temporary only to be followed with something horrible. It took a lot of conscious effort to reduce these automatic thought responses, and one tool that helped me to do it was *meditation.*

I actually learned meditation and contemplative practices from a former monk. One thing I've learned in life—if you want to learn how to master anything, go to a master. To understand and better control my own thoughts, I sought out a person who knows and practices exactly what I wished to learn.

Meditation is a free and easy practice that anyone can do. Meditation is not about controlling your thoughts; it's to stop letting them control you. If you are not happy with the people, experiences, and feelings you're attracting in your life, give it a try. If you are happy with the people, experiences, and feelings you are attracting in your life, give it a try. If you are in between, give it a try.

I've been meditating for the past thirty years and I first began in five minute increments. Thanks to the Internet, there are many practitioners available to get you started and keep you connected. Meditation, like exercise, requires an ongoing commitment to experience its benefits. *Be aware of your dominant thoughts as they become your life experiences!*

Insight Two, The Law of Attraction

Are you clear on experiences you want to attract or do you push against things you don't want? Yes, the law of attraction is as real as the law of gravity and available to every living form. All living things focus on their evolution; even plants depend upon thoughts around them to continue fine tuning their growth.

As previously mentioned we attract to us whatever we continually think about. Do you deliberately create your life or is your life a series of random events? Do you follow your own path or the paths of others? Do the things you want in life have any corresponding doubt factors?

Are your feelings consistent with your thoughts and words? Think about it—do you want people to care about you? If so, do you spend time showing people you care? Like attracts like. Whatever you want in your life, focus on that area; then give it away to others and you will receive it—it is a universal principle, a law.

Remember to focus on what you want, not on what you do not want. Resisting something only reinforces its intensity and brings more of the something "not wanted" to you.

For years I ran to rescue people from their own behaviors and failed every single time. People I attracted into my life were people who needed help and would not help themselves. Why?

Because I was programmed this way from childhood where I learned survival skills. Perhaps that is why I became an ICU nurse so I could continue to save people. Instead of focusing on what I wanted, healthy relationships, I focused on what I didn't want—train wrecks. I know many of you can identify with my own problematic attractions.

When I began to study and understand the law of attraction, I learned to focus on what I did want and moved away from the not wanted. As humans we often find it easier to list and discuss what is not going well, turning to negative thinking. Yet, resisting just reinforces what you don't want; the more you fight against it, the more it continues and controls you.

Why do you think news is so full of the negative events? Because negativity sells. Think about it. Do you listen to the negative only to complain that everything is so negative? Just stop paying attention to it.

Write down at least three things you do not want in your life such as sickness, a job loss, or higher taxes. Instead of focusing on what you don't want, turn each one into a statement of what you do want. For example, instead of "I don't want to be sick," turn it around to "I am well and am getting better every day." *It's impossible to get what you want when you push against the unwanted.*

Insight Three, Words Reflect Emotions

Do you think about words you use? Are you aware of their power? Words spring from thoughts and thoughts are nutrition for your mind. Your thoughts create certain feelings and your feelings cause you to say things and behave in certain ways—realities that substantiate a whole self-fulfilling prophecy.

We all know people who remain totally disconnected from their feelings—they don't understand how to tap into them let alone make changes. Yet, a simple change in thoughts makes a profound difference in feelings.

If you want to tap into how you feel, pay attention to the words you use. Do you hear or listen to your words? For example, think of the difference between "I can't do it now," as opposed to "I choose not to do that now," or "I have taken on a great deal of work and choose not to add anything more at this time." Try this one: "Things happen to me," or "I make things happen!"

The difference in these approaches is the difference between being a victim or feeling empowered. A simple change in your words has an enormous impact on how you feel. How do you feel when you say the above sentences aloud?

Think about the words you use when describing any situation. Ask yourself a question and then pay attention to your response. Or better yet, engage in a discussion with a friend and pay attention to words and phrases you use. You will be surprised.

Our self-talk emanates from thoughts and is then expressed in our spoken words. What would your wardrobe be if your words wrapped around you like clothing? I had a friend who always apologized for everything that went wrong around her. It was as if she were apologizing for her right to exist.

Your words mirror your thoughts and feelings, so remain aware of your vocabulary. *Your words are powerful and reflect your emotional state.*

Insight Four, Life Is An Echo

If you get experiences you do not enjoy, do you examine experiences you give out? What you send out into the world in words and actions returns to you; in short, you reap what you sow. In some cultures this phenomenon is referred to as "Karma." Karma is the intent and actions of a person (cause) that influences the future of that individual (effect); good intent and good deeds contribute to good karma while bad intent and bad deeds contribute to bad karma.

Karma is a law of cause and effect by which we create our destiny with our thoughts, words, and deeds—actions in our life that vibrate in eternity.

With the currency of your karmic actions you purchase and create your life experiences—good, bad, pleasant, and unpleasant. To receive happiness, peace, love, and friendship, be happy, peaceful, loving, and a faithful friend.

Think about a time you may have said something or hurt someone. Was it intentional? Did someone hurt you in a similar way in your life? Think about a time you gave money and then found money you didn't know you had. These are examples of how you reap what you sow.

Years ago, I grew to loathe the work I was doing. As a result, more loathing experiences kept coming my way. I finally walked away from that work as I was becoming someone I didn't like. *If you get experiences you do not enjoy, examine the experiences you give out.*

Insight Five, Recurring Life Patterns

Do you ever take time to examine your life? An unexamined life will break down and what you do from that point forward matters. As you think so you act, and unconscious actions over time become habits or patterns in our lives.

Life patterns differ from dominate thought patterns as they are situations you find yourself in over and over again. Kind of like *déjà vu* or the experience of "I've been here before." Repeating life patterns are often unconscious until you realize you just cannot do these same things over and over and expect different results.

This awareness often comes when your life is broken and you are broken open; a time when you're forced to become more introspective. Changing your life patterns is not easy. In fact, most of us change only when the pain of our old patterns becomes untenable.

If you are unsure of your own life patterns, keep a diary for a week or a month to monitor your behaviors and responses. Look at areas that repeat and how you feel about them.

For me, it was overextending myself over and over again. I have a close friend who used to say to me all the time "are you overextending yourself?" We met when I was working full time, going to school full time, starting a regional association, and going through a divorce. Get the picture? It was a life pattern I repeated until I learned to say no.

We have no life maps; only a sense of direction. So determine what makes you happy and brings you joy. Then hold yourself in that vibrational place to line up with what you want—it should feel great. So many people have given up on themselves sacrificing their own wants and dreams on the altar of another's ambition. Are you aware when you step into a repeating pattern and wonder, "Why am I here again?"

Back in the 1960s, there was a television show "Lost in Space." A primitive robot would wave his arms and shout, "warning, warning" if something negative was around or its radar detected it could lead to danger. We all need this radar in our lives. *An unexamined life will break down and what you do from that point forward matters.*

Insight Six, When Life Doesn't Fit Anymore

When you realize life doesn't fit anymore, do you have the courage to make the needed changes? This one is a big one. Do you have an overarching, aching feeling that goes beyond a current thought, problem or situation—so much so that your life needs to change, that you need to significantly change!

It's much more than a project going south or a relationship tanking. It's greater than realizing ongoing life patterns and actually emerges from ignoring them. It's a time you realize that nothing is working; an unhappiness of repeating life patterns coupled with a painful awareness that something needs to dramatically change. It is often when you reach bottom.

Many times we force ourselves to stay the course because it seems prudent. Maybe you've invested a lot of time and effort into creating something, or you've put in years to get to where you are now.

Consider an area in your life where walking away from someone or something can appear downright crazy to people close to you or even seem crazy to you. Write about it and think about your options.

For me it happened in my mid-sixties. I found that my life had drifted so far away from the person I was. Nothing was working and I was bored and miserable; in fact, I was walking through a Dark Night of the Soul. My life fell apart and I had to make some significant changes. More on this Dark Night experience in Chapter Eight. *When your life isn't working have the courage to make the needed changes.*

Insight Seven, Run Your Own Race

Do you find yourself explaining yourself to others? In a world filled with perfectly curated lives streaming across various media, the constant pressure to compare yourself to others can be overwhelming. It's so easy to get wrapped up in what other people are doing, and feel like you have to compete. Whether it's with jobs, relationships, or life in general, just because someone else follows a particular path doesn't mean it's for you.

Einstein once said, *"Everybody is a genius. But if you judge a fish by its ability to climb a tree, it will live its whole life believing that it is stupid."*

Don't try to catch up to others because you want their success. Use your own talents and run your own race. Go after your own story, stay in your own lane, and chase whatever energizes you. Do you even know what energizes you? Ask yourself, what activities get me into the flow—a place where I feel my best? A space where time passes by and I do not notice? Here is your path and what you are meant to do in life. If you have to explain yourself to others, you are off course.

If you find yourself bored with life, your interests and skills may be higher than your current challenges; you can do them effortlessly and you are not challenged. If you feel overly stressed in life, you may be challenged beyond your abilities; either increase your skill levels or move on to something else.

For most of my life, it was always about building the next new thing. Why? For me, innovation energizes and regulation is a death knell. Once anything gets to be routine, I'm on the move.

Go for the big ask! Most people ask for too little not too much. What are your burning desires? What actually pulls you through the mud is the vision you had when you began your quest. Write down two or three activities that energize you—activities you can stay with for hours. *Life is much simpler when you stop explaining yourself to others and just live a life that works for you.*

CHAPTER TWO—POWER OF BELIEFS

Gandhi articulated his wisdom when he said, *"Your beliefs become your thoughts, your thoughts become your words, your words become your actions, your actions become your habits, your habits become your values, your values become your destiny."* Realize that behind everything you say is a thought and behind every thought is a belief.

Insight Eight, Deeply Rooted Beliefs

Think about your long held beliefs? Do you know that beliefs form your character and they are often unconscious? Have you ever wondered where your beliefs originated? They don't just appear randomly—they reflect your long held truths about health, love, work, family as well as politics, religion and money.

Beliefs begin in childhood and expand over time. We learned basic beliefs as young children and created experiences that matched those beliefs throughout life. Are you someone who clings to personal beliefs resisting other points of view?

Our beliefs seed our character. Some remain indestructible while others are thin around the base and can be broken easily. Think about a belief you hold today. Is it one from childhood or one that has adapted or changed over the years? How have your beliefs influenced your behaviors over the years?

Realize that personal beliefs can entrench, may become rooted in negativity and/or become destructive. We witnessed this reality through the pandemic with entrenchment driven by political discourse.

So many people stopped listening to others' viewpoints focusing only on information that matched their own beliefs. Rather than examine truth versus rumor, some of us held firm to our own ways and refused to allow other viewpoints into our world.

Beliefs also drive our self-worth. Are you someone who believes your worth comes from another's validation—what others believe you to be rather than who you believe yourself to be? *Long held beliefs form your character and are often unconscious.*

Insight Nine, Emotions Reflect Beliefs

Do you continuously try to change things around you to feel better? Try feeling better first and witness how things around you change. Think of your thoughts as weather patterns and your emotions as barometers. Who would you be without your emotions? If the sum total of all your experiences makes up the tapestry of your life, it is your emotions that give this tapestry its color. While words are language of the mind, actions are language of the body and emotions are language of the soul.

What are your emotional set points? Do you tend to close up, shut down or blow up? Have you learned to maximize positive emotions (desire, faith, love, enthusiasm, hope) and minimize negative ones (fear, jealousy, hatred, revenge, greed, anger)? Or do you maximize negative emotions while minimizing the positive? If you are feeling bad, what you are thinking? Holding in emotions only weakens the body.

To offset this one, try having a kid's temper tantrum—scream in your car or punch out a pillow to release stress and frustration or just have a good cry.

Crying removes toxins from the body and is a safety valve to prevent emotional overdoses. If you are feeling good, keep thinking that way and expand those emotions. Make it a personal priority to feel good and believe in yourself. *Stop trying to change things to feel better; feel better and things around you change.*

Insight Ten, Beliefs Become Biology

Do you know how your thoughts and beliefs forge a relationship with wellness or illness? Your body's cells are not in competition with one another for the most resources; instead, they work collaboratively and cooperatively allowing multi-celled organisms to evolve and thrive in changing environments.

Our beliefs, expressed in thoughts and emotions, influence our cells in ways we're just beginning to understand. Just think of the placebo effect as a case in point! The placebo effect is when our mind holds something to be true (a belief), it then becomes true.

Personal beliefs held long enough become programmed into our biology. I have seen people with positive beliefs recover from surgery sooner or move on after a devastating loss faster.

When we stifle emotions they embed into the body. Negative and toxic thoughts increase stress levels and lower immune function. For example, grief affects immune function and does not end when any services are over. We know the pandemic brought stages of grief that never ended with continuing losses on multiple fronts. This unconscious stress wreaks havoc on the body, and it is well studied that long term grief, anger, and resentment is associated with developing cancers.

Think of something that brings you down, such as a job loss or a diagnosis of diabetes and pay attention to how your body feels. Can you feel your energy change? Now think of something that brings you joy, such as getting a new job you love or meeting a friend you haven't seen in years, and experience this emotion in your body. Feel the difference.

The body obeys the mind's operational commands, whether they're deliberately chosen or they are automatically expressed. At the bidding of prolonged negative thought patterns, the body sinks rapidly into disease and decay; at the command of glad and positive thoughts, it becomes more energized and radiates magnificence. *Your thoughts and beliefs forge a relationship with wellness or illness.*

Insight Eleven, Your Life From the Inside Out

Do you seek validation outside yourself? Millions of people can believe in you, yet none of it matters if you do not believe in yourself. Beliefs are as unique to each person as individual fingerprints, and while you may share similar families and cultures each one of you has a different composition of values and beliefs. Are you aware of belief systems operating in your world? Do you believe in your own abilities and in yourself?

Inner beliefs reflect deep seated perceptions, attitudes, and values that drive decisions—oftentimes unconsciously. Do you automatically follow a recommendation? Do you continuously try to fit yourself into boxes that only make you miserable? Do you believe in your own abilities and talents?

Self-doubt reaches its highest peak in perfectionism. You set such ambitious standards for yourself that you never move forward. What are you afraid of—rejection, not being good enough or looking foolish? Remember, once you've accepted your flaws no one can use them against you.

Write a statement in the positive about something you desire such as "I have a new job that uses my talents and I am happy." Start with "I am____ or I have____." Refer to this statement each day for a month and feel how this statement aligns with your beliefs. Believe in your own ability to make it happen.

Start affirming what you want and state it in positive and current terms. Check yourself to ensure you're affirming positively without any negativity slipping in. Do you believe you will never graduate or that you won't have enough money to retire? Or do you affirm that you finish what you set out to do and there is always enough. *Millions of people can believe in you, yet none of it matters if you do not believe in yourself.*

Insight Twelve, Your Life From the Outside In

How do you view your body? Your body is not who you are. When you look into a mirror who do you see—an aging sixty-year-old man or a vibrant sixty-year-old man? Do you see your hair color, wrinkles, or overweight torso as pluses or minuses? Just talk to any older person whether he is fifty or ninety, and you will get the same response—a younger person is still alive inside.

Everything and everyone in our lives is a mirror of who we are inside. Yet, we don't realize how much *stuff* from the outside we let into our inner world such as opinions, judgments and recommendations. We see it on screens, hear it from family and absorb it from our friends on a continuing basis.

Look into the mirror and look deeply into your inner self. Look into your own eyes and keep looking until you feel good or have to look away. Can you look at yourself closely without feeling discomfort? Are you comfortable with your face, body and the essence that is you? Can you tell yourself that you love yourself? Self-confidence and self-love are superpowers. *Your body is not who you are.*

Insight Thirteen, Reality of Expectations

Do you believe in what you desire? Any desire with a corresponding doubt factor will go nowhere. You may desire that new car but do not believe you deserve it. Expectation is where your desires and beliefs intersect. Expectations are the root of all disappointment when your beliefs do not align with your definition of reality.

Too often we set out toward a goal but inside we're unsure of our commitment to it. We expect to produce a great result but inside there is doubt. Maybe you really do not believe in it at all or want nothing to do with it. You may desire to finish something but to what extent? You can never meet any expectations when desire and belief oppose one another.

Write down something you desire and then beside it write down any doubts you have about it. For example, I am earning $200,000 a year. Beside it write any corresponding doubt factors such as "I'm not good enough" or "things like that never happen to me." Which one of these statements is stronger, the desire or the doubt?

Remember what you think about, talk about, believe strongly about, feel intensely about, you can bring about. Why? Because you expect it to happen; you believe it will happen; you *just know* it will happen.

For fifteen years I believed in building a more responsive model for elder services. I had some successes but also many disappointments. As service quality diminished around me focusing more on money than care services, I found myself surrounded by companies engaged in a race to the bottom. I began to doubt my own model until I realized I had planted my fruits in toxic soil. Then I knew what to do and moved on. *Any desire with a corresponding doubt factor will go nowhere.*

Insight Fourteen, Practice Gratitude

How appreciative are you for what you have? Happiness arrives when you appreciate your world today. Do you know wealthy people who are unhappy people? They only want more rather than enjoying what has been given to them. Both abundance and scarcity are inner states—abundance manifests with a sense of appreciation and gratefulness and scarcity through criticism and fear.

Acknowledging the good already in your life is a foundation for any and all abundance. When you appreciate all you have, more of it flows into your life.

If you are complaining you don't have enough, more of the "not enough" will flow to you. Whatever you think people are withholding from you, just give it to them. When you start giving, you start receiving.

Intention is important here. If you *only give* to receive, it doesn't work. Get yourself in a state of flow where income and outputs move through you easily and this flow brings you joy. When you are grateful, the vibration of appreciation shows up more in your life.

Be clear on anything relating to gratitude, such as a relationship, an event, a job, a home, a car, anything! Feel grateful before it arrives and be thankful for what you have before you actually have it. Start each day with gratitude.

Never regret a day in your life. Ask yourself, if today was last day of my life how would I want to spend it mentally? Remember that good days bring happiness, bad days offer experience, the worst days provide lessons and the best days cement memories. List at least three things you are grateful to have in life each day—be specific. *Happiness arrives when you appreciate what you have.*

CHAPTER THREE—POWER OF INTEGRITY

While the first two chapters looked inward, this chapter examines how you show yourself to the world. Personal integrity enables you to achieve your goals and live your best life. It is the ability to be honest with yourself, accept your limitations, and follow through on your word no matter what.

Having integrity means that you live in accordance with your deepest values, you're honest with people, and you keep your word. Integrity is a highly valued trait for anyone as it defines who you are and brings you self-respect and the respect of others in your orbit.

Insight Fifteen, A Positive Brand

What do you stand for? Your brand is who you are, the values you embrace, and how you express those values. Personal integrity is doing the right thing even when it's hard. Many people only do what they are supposed to because they know someone is watching. True integrity is abiding by the rules because you know that it's the right thing to do and over time defines your personal brand.

Personal brand springs from motive and intent—it answers the question, why? *Why* did you do this or think that? Can you write your own personal brand statement? How do people know you and refer to you? How do you refer to yourself? Are you a class act? Brand is not about career only; it is about how you show up in your life. Can you write your own obituary of a life well lived and live your life to match it?

If you are doing something you feel bad about, stop doing it. Your character is developed and revealed by tests, and life is one test after another. *Your brand is who you are, what you stand for, the values you embrace, and how you express those values.*

Insight Sixteen, Your Personal Truth

What is your truth? When standing in your own truth, you do not need validation from others. Your core values are basic convictions about what you believe is right, good, or bad; they play a key role in any decision. Without a set of core values, you drift aimlessly in life and any wind blows you. These "emotional rules" govern your behaviors and your attitudes, which in turn affect your choices and commitments.

Commitments we make or don't make either develop us or destroy us. Politicians come to mind here as so many of them say one thing and do another. They lack core values or a sense of themselves. This is one reason so many of us have lost respect for governments.

A lack of core values, or a sense of personal truth, is why people easily follow others and let other people define them. Remember, if you cannot be who you are you are not on your right path. When living your own truth you feel good even if external events are negative. When you are at one with yourself—your authentic self—you are unstoppable.

If there is too much heavy lifting to bring someone or something to your level of truth, let go; do not let it drag you down. People who lack the clarity, courage or determination to follow their own dreams will often find ways to discourage yours.

Being authentic is not so much about changing what you do but shifting your attitude toward who you are. It takes courage and openness to remain authentic. Don't confuse knowing yourself with knowing *about yourself.* That 5000-page dossier about your life is only the content of your mind and conditioned by the past.

Sometimes at that fork in the road you know exactly which road to take. At that fork, taking the right road for you is the one that is often most difficult. Think back to a time when you faced a personal choice: Did you follow your own truth or listen to someone else? Take a piece of paper and write down the things you wanted to do but didn't do. *When standing in your own truth, there is no need to seek validation from others.*

Insight Seventeen, Intuition As A Guide

Do you believe you're intuitive? It's true, we all have an intuitive sense as an internal guide. Intuition is following your own instincts. If you align with your own truth and live with integrity, your ability to understand surfaces without the need for conscious reasoning. We all possess this inner instinct and its abilities. For some, it is a groomed filter on how to move through life; for others, it is dull and considered something only other people possess. Think of a time when you didn't follow your "gut" and how that one turned out for you.

Some call intuition a "hunch;" others call it a "genius" or a "muse." I call it "my life guide." By harnessing my internal *guide*, I tap the ideas, thoughts and knowledge of higher states of being! How do you access your inner guide? Think of a decision you need to make now or in the near future. It could be a simple one such as where to vacation or a more

significant one such as a marriage. Do you turn in and listen to that inner guide or go right for someone else's opinion of what to do?

During the pandemic holidays, my family and I questioned whether to gather with others or take a more cautious approach. My instincts were strong about following public health guidelines and I did. When we arrived, there was a group of people stating the pandemic was a hoax, they would not social distance and there was not a mask to be found. So three of us sat outside on the porch. From that gathering, four people got sick and one person died. *We all have intuition as an internal guide.*

Insight Eighteen, Make It Better or Move On

How often do you berate yourself over an error? Are you able to let go of a mistake but learn the lesson? We've all made errors in judgment and with our actions. The question is how long do you hold onto that mistake?

Do you help others in certain situations? Does that help ever shift from trying to make it better for them to them *draining you* too much? Do they only focus on the problem showing no interest in solving it? Does the problem go on and on as the person does not want to improve, and the situation cannot get better?

If you cannot improve the situation move on quietly. If the situation is toxic or corrupt move on quickly and do not look back. Stop planning to do it. Stop thinking about doing it. Stop contemplating doing it. Stop wishing you were doing it. Just do it—whatever your "it" is.

You may fail but you'll learn from that failure. One experience for me was with a musical band. Why couldn't it get anywhere? There was one person who lacked talent and while he had passion, he couldn't sing or play an instrument. Others in the group knew the problem but said nothing and would do nothing. For me, I couldn't make it better and the entire situation was draining me. I gracefully exited.

Take a piece of paper and divide it into two columns—label one column "energizes" and the other "drains." Down the left side list five consistent activities in your life. Then place a check in the "energizes" column or the "drains" column. This exercise is quite insightful.

Look at the draining areas and be willing to let go of areas that suck the life out of you. *Let go of the mistake but learn the lesson.*

Insight Nineteen, Stay the Course

Do you accept reality or do you tend to live in fantasy? Maturity is living with the tension between what is real and what is ideal. It isn't easy balancing the two, especially in these times. However, staying the course requires you accept what is and keep commitments.

Commitment and staying the course depends on your values. What do you value? Family, health, money, prestige, titles? Laurie believed in spending time with her children and keeping them active, yet worked two jobs and didn't have any time to spend with her children. Her value of time with her children was in conflict with her value of financially supporting her children.

Show me someone's bank account and calendar, and I will show you what that person values. How we spend our money, and our time, shows the world our values.

What are your values about money—What do you spend and what do you not spend? Do you buy beer or health club memberships? What are your values about time? Do you have balance or exist on a treadmill with little time for yourself and others? What are your values about health? Do your health habits and lifestyles support your words?

We all long for that ideal life and may think we are living it. If we are not [living ideal life], we may want to but do not believe we can. We pretend and fake an existence between the real and the ideal. I see social media sites full of people pushing out stories of ideal family lives when their reality is far from it.

Longing for the ideal while criticizing the real is a sign of immaturity. Settling for the real and not striving for the ideal is complacency. *Maturity is living with the tension between the real and the ideal.*

Insight Twenty, Go It Alone

Have you ever done something completely alone, without support or encouragement just because you knew it was right for you? There are times in life it is better to be a lonely lion than a popular sheep.

Many of us have a vision for our lives. Yet vision without action is merely a dream. If there are things you want to do and you're waiting for someone else to do them with you, they never happen. Maybe you're terrified to take action. You're afraid to apply for that job, you're afraid to ask for that date, you're afraid to jump out of your comfort zone. The truth of the matter is that you have nothing to lose.

Think of something you're afraid to do. Now ask yourself, "What's the worst that could happen?" Then after each fear, write *so what*? Keep dividing it down until you get to the real reason for staying stuck.

In my twenties, I moved to California with three other people to start a new life. After an eventful cross-country trip, we arrived and then everyone went home. I decided to stay even if it meant I was alone. I almost went back with them but asked myself "why was I afraid?"

My answer, being alone. I then asked myself, "what's so frightening about being alone?" The answer, I don't know anyone here; what if something happens? I then said to myself, "you started many new things where you didn't know anyone." I then realized I had already met people I liked and it would be OK.

Almost always, asking this question will make you realize that you need to just do it. It moves you from the viewpoint of another obstacle to one of another challenge and answers the question, "how much do I really want it?"

Do you follow along even if it goes against who you are? Does the approval of others become a mirror that defines you? Do you depend on others to give you a sense of self? Tough questions to answer but ones that will help you grow and become happier. *Sometimes it's better to be a lonely lion than a popular sheep.*

Insight Twenty-One, The "Why" Behind the Action

Do you ever ask yourself why you do the things you do? What incentives lie behind the things you think and speak? Answering the question "why" connects us to who we are and reveals intentions behind what we do and how we do it.

Young children constantly ask "why," and ask that same question repeatedly until they know *why* they have to do something or *why* things are a certain way. They seek to understand the world they live in. *Why? But why?* And adults typically answer with "because I said so."

Ask and the door will be open! What is your ask? Move from merely wanting something to knowing WHY you want something. The reasons for your "ask "define your purpose and give meaning, direction, and reason to any action. Stop spinning around like a gyroscope—always busy but going nowhere.

Ask yourself *why* you took that job, married that person, live in a certain area. Be honest with yourself and it opens unconscious drivers for past decisions.

Decades ago I struggled in a career. I was bored and unchallenged yet this career paid well. These conflicting incentives kept me stuck until I answered my own question "why." It focused me and then forced me to let go and move on. I went out on my own and started a new business, something different. Why? Because innovation energizes me and routine is a death knell. *Know the intention behind anything you think, say or do.*

FORCE TWO—FILTERING

With so much pollution put out over the airwaves, in print, in social circles and on social media, how sharp are your filters when seeking out and letting in information and experiences? Do you have methods to screen fact from fiction and precision from propaganda?

This second force takes a look at your internal filters, the externals in your life, and how you screen information through personal beliefs and values. Do you accept information as presented or do you think about it before you act?

The question here is about "what to leave in and what to leave out?" These next few chapters dive into personal responsibility and how you filter the world around you.

This section includes *Chapters Four through Seven* and takes a look at the power of choosing, preparing, and making decisions. Insight *twenty-two through forty-nine* cover areas of responsibility, planning, health and wealth.

CHAPTER FOUR—POWER OF CHOICE

How you live life springs from deeply rooted beliefs that continually filter information around you. We make choices from information we do or do not let in. Yet onslaughts of misinformation, disinformation, fake news, and conspiracy push way too much fiction into every life.

We all need to sharpen our filters before we take action. What is your approach? Do you readily accept or do you think before acting?

Insight Twenty-Two, Be Responsible

Do you take responsibility for your life? Do you consciously make choices and accept results your choices bring? Know that you *are* 100 percent responsible for your life—your achievements, your failures, the quality of your relationships, the states of your health, your physical fitness, your wealth, your debts and your career.

Too often we blame others for our lot in life and live as victims. Do you still blame your parents, friends, co-workers, the economy or a lack of money for your problems? Or do you take a position that you have the power to get it right and can produce the life you want? Realize that the past is over and has no power in your present.

To live responsibly requires personal boundaries—boundaries that filter effectively. Are your boundaries rigid, porous or healthy? A person who always keeps others at a distance (whether emotionally, physically, or otherwise) has rigid boundaries. They won't allow anything to flow in or out, like having a blocked filter.

People with porous boundaries tend to get too involved with others becoming one with the yoke. They allow themselves to be manipulated and can suffer the consequences. If you've ever let someone make you feel guilty, you may have porous personal boundaries. Once you are an adult, no one runs your life—you do.

People with healthy boundaries tend to share personal information in the most appropriate manner (not over or under share). And most importantly, they learn to say "no" and know how to accept it when others say "no."

On a scale of one to ten, how healthy are your boundaries? Do you have a strong sense of self and take responsibility for your life? *You are responsible for the choices you make and the results they bring.*

Insight Twenty-Three, Perception Creates Reality

People with the same outward experience do not have the same inner experience. We are all hardwired differently. Neurologists estimate that two million or more signals come into your brain every second, yet only three or four of these signals actually register in awareness. Why? Your perception filters these signals, and only the ones that have meaning to you get through.

How we frame current situations arises from past experiences. We attach meaning in our lives through our mind interacting with the world as we know it. For example, the birth of a child can be a blessing or another mouth to feed; a job loss can be a burden or a wakeup call; a sports injury can be the end of a career or the beginning of another.

The way you see your life shapes your life; when you change the way you look at things, things you look at do change. Two men looked through prison bars; one saw mud and the other saw stars.

Think of a time when you were frustrated and could not do anything about it. Did the situation escalate or did you just let it go and accept it for what it was? For example, a traffic jam can be a source of anger or a time to turn up the music and relax. Nothing external changes, just your response.

Two people can be side by side and witness an event. The meaning that each person gives to this event will be different. Think of your siblings—you all grew up in the same household but took away different experiences. *People with same outward experiences do not have the same inner experiences.*

Insight Twenty-Four, Information Integrity

Do you accept information at face value or do you check it out first? How do you filter facts, fakes, disinformation or conspiracy theories? People pay attention to information that supports personal views and dismiss information that challenges them. How you filter information, and then act, is a critical component to any choice.

Exposed to hundreds of cable channels, thousands of newspapers, countless radio shows, limitless websites and unbounded social media platforms, people tweet, post, upload and download information every minute without any thought to what it is, who is sending it and if it's factual. With twenty-four-hour television news stations, you have access to the latest news in real time, anytime.

But is it accurate? Is it unbiased? Is it harmful? Certain information genres surged during the pandemic and continue today: misinformation, disinformation and conspiracy theories.

Misinformation: People post misinformation to their websites, send it through social media, and spread it to people known and unknown. Most people who simply share information are not trying to misinform. Instead they're raising a concern, trying to make sense of conflicting information, or seeking answers to specific questions.

While not intentional, this information-sharing needs to be vetted or at least questioned. Do you know that most online support groups aren't monitored and stories and advice may not be accurate? If that advice is ever retracted, you may never know.

Most misinformation is unintentional but can be spread deliberately with malicious intention to trick people for financial gain or political advantage. This information exchange is known as "disinformation."

Disinformation: People spread disinformation to mislead, manipulate; or promote propaganda. It's hard to trace its source or to determine its credibility, and it's easy to find any fake expert if you pay enough.

For example, certain medications promoted as "cures" during the pandemic were quite dangerous to humans. Unscrupulous sources push out fake information as fact knowing that few people check it out. They do it to capture your attention and distract you from any truth. These campaigns create alternate realities that push conspiracy theories.

Conspiracy Theories: Conspiracy theories advance stories that explain an event by concocting a secret plot that is often politically motivated. Conspiracy theories are not rooted in reality and create alternate facts and views that are simply made up. Why do so many people drop into these rabbit holes of disinformation and conspiracy theories? Many people get pulled into these streams of fantasy as they try and make sense of their world. Be careful.

Next time you read a news clip, receive a tweet, or review information ask yourself, "How do I know the information is accurate?" Then answer your own question. *Learn to filter factual from fake information.*

Insight Twenty-Five, Sourcing the Source

Do you consider the source of advice or news stories? Do you think about tracing essential information to its *source* to ensure it's credible? Accurate, credible, and timely information guides your choices, changes behaviors, and impacts results. Your first question concerning any piece of information, "What is the actual source of this information?" or "Where does this information originate?" Be aware that media and politicians are ***not*** sources.

Know that major funding sources for advertisements (especially network TV) are food and drug companies. Their tactics influence you to demand their products, services, or medications. These tactics work well creating billion-dollar industries at the expense of your health.

To find where information and recommendations originate, go deep. There are too many experts without any expertise pushing conspiracy and propaganda. Just because someone has MD after his name does not make him an expert on the subject. *Remember that the expert is not the source.* They take information and manipulate it so you will think differently.

Think about it. When you enter a search term online, do you get hundreds if not thousands of results? Many of these results are just lead generators—results that only point you to more *experts without expertise*—all trying to sell something you do not need. Worse, they pull you into some type of scam.

Has this situation happened to you? You respond to an 800 number and get inundated with insurance agents or sellers of everything from where to put a parent to how to buy your food. When you search the Internet for information, do you check to see if the returns are labelled as "ads" or the real deal?

Have you been the victim of a scam? Follow the money, find the source and it will lead you to the truth. *Trace information to its source to ensure it is credible.*

Insight Twenty-Six, Technology—A Super Spreader

Will we live for humanity or for technology? While convenient and accessible, technology easily delivers toxic content. Media everywhere create banquets of information, yet we starve for any meaning. Every day new devices, advances in products, apps and social media sites are released into markets. Do you live your life tuned into your phone, media, texts, emails and respond within minutes? Are you obsessed with technology and spend your days looking at a screen to stay connected?

In addition to various media, each medium expands its reach. For example, television now offers more than five hundred channels, and the number of new websites doubles each day. You can call a friend from a computer, access the Web from a TV, and capture a video with your smartphone. Today's media bombards us with the latest news and findings in 30-second sound bites which leaves too many of us with only part of the message.

There is also a dark side to Web-based information. The Internet is loaded with misleading and false information. A flashy website may attract you, but can be full of false and fake facts. Before you act, think. There is no regulation for advertising on the Internet, and individuals and companies can promote and promise anything. *While convenient and accessible, technology easily delivers toxic content.*

Insight Twenty-Seven, Recognize Barriers to Trust

Do you know that deeply rooted beliefs affect how you approach facts and make choices? When we are unsure or afraid, we tend to seek out information that will comfort and make us whole. All of us imagine the worst when we do not know what is true.

The pandemic created many casualties when it came to accurate information. Why? Because we stopped believing in experts and turned to anyone who supported our beliefs. As the pandemic wore on, *multiple barriers* expanded around information, sources, and messengers that eroded our trust.

The first trust barrier, so many media outlets lean either conservative or liberal, and their views filter information from politics to a public health crisis. This barrier becomes problematic because of "selection bias" or selective exposure—the idea that the more choices available, the more we seek sources that reinforce our beliefs. For example, conservatives tend to gravitate toward conservative media, and liberals tend to seek out liberal media. We all have the tendency to dismiss information that does not align with our own beliefs.

The second trust barrier, media or governments get things wrong. They convey incorrect information which may be retracted in a statement, but misinformation is circulating. You may never see the retraction and may continue to share this misinformation as if it were completely fact-based. Maybe you don't trust media or governments at all and tune it all out.

The third trust barrier, sponsors pay big bucks for disinformation and drive conspiracy theories. Just look at how many news media are sponsored by drug and food companies.

The fourth trust barrier, media promote conflicting information that confuses people. During the COVID-19 pandemic, recommendations continued to evolve and change as doctors and researchers learned more about the disease. The importance of consistent communication and messaging cannot be overemphasized.

The problem with each of these barriers is constant confusion leads people to believe in hoaxes and conspiracy theories as they try to make sense of their worlds. We all seek ways to package information into actions that make sense to us.

When I was an undergraduate, I enrolled in a debate class. One of the assignments was to research a topic I felt strongly about and then argue the opposite opinion. I learned so much so long ago from that one activity. The biggest lesson was to at least research and hear out the other side before digging down on my own opinions. Consider a belief about something important to you. Can you respect another opinion, listen to a different viewpoint and stay calm? *Our deep rooted beliefs affect how we approach facts.*

Insight Twenty-Eight, When in Doubt, Check It Out

Do you know the importance of learning how to learn rather than just what to learn? Knowing how to learn employs critical thinking skills; knowing what to learn uses memorization techniques. *Critical thinking is the ability to deliberate clearly and rationally, understanding the logical connection between ideas.* When you have a question, instead of assuming do you seek out answers? This exercise is not as simple as it seems.

First, observe and think about what you read and/or what is said. *Second,* analyze the facts, consider the source (where the information originates). Does it feel right, ring true to you or generate a hostile and negative emotion such as fear? *Third,* form conclusions based on facts that align with who you are. *Fourth,* apply the solution to the question or problem you are trying to solve. It's a simple process to understand but not so easy to implement. Most people just react.

Do you feel a sense of urgency to react to and/or share emotionally charged misinformation with others, enabling it to spread quickly and go "viral?" Are you able to slow down and wait it out—few decisions are actual emergencies? Do you think about what you share and how you make choices? Is it true and what is truth? *Focus on how to learn more than what to learn.*

CHAPTER FIVE—POWER OF PREPARATION

We create so much of our own misery through a lack of preparation. We deny a problem exists, delay a response or delete its relevance. We then scramble to respond to a full blown crisis that grew from this lack of preparation.

Insight Twenty-Nine, Chasms of Neglect and Panic

Do you plan or do you just allow things to happen? Can you identify one neglected area in your life? These neglected areas quickly become threats that eventually force awareness and action. Think about this fact—the recent pandemic had been predicted for years before it actually arrived, yet little to no preparation took place until it was too late.

This cycle of neglect, stalked by panic, follows a typical pattern: First announce an unseen emergency, next approve immediate funding to respond to the crisis, then follow it with commitments to fix these problems in the immediate aftermath.

Once the emergency passes, the support wanes and attention shifts elsewhere. Why? Most of us are not conditioned to plan; we deal with the present crisis, complain we didn't know it was coming, and then make hasty and expensive decisions. We do it all the time. Yet none of us individually wants what we do collectively.

Another example of this neglect/panic cycle is avoiding realities of worldwide aging populations. We've known for decades that the number of people over sixty-five would outpace the number of people under eighteen by 2030. And yet we continue to deny this reality is coming? Well it's not coming, it's here!

Another example is climate change. For decades, scientists have cited climate change as a culprit destroying natural resources. However, denial reigns supreme despite the reality of raging storms, constant destruction, receding access to water, and massive migrations.

Another example is a ballooning federal debt. Debt burdens continue to mushroom yet remain ignored because it's not today's problem. This book published in the fall of 2022; we are in an economic recession that many people still deny.

As individuals, we live cycles of neglect and panic; then when any personal crisis hits, we use an approach of *ready, fire, aim!!* Think about it. How do you plan? Do you wait for a crisis that will change life in minutes? What now? Wait, what? Is that your response?

Poor planning or no planning only creates bigger problems. Get clear and get started today with one small step. *Identify one neglected area in your life and develop a simple plan.*

Insight Thirty, Allow for Detours

How many times do you set goals you don't achieve? Once you decide on a specific course, how flexible do you remain in allowing for detours? A decision, a goal, or a New Year's resolution is not a success, it is not the destination. These declarations do not create the motivation or action needed because they are only desires at this point.

A dream without a plan is just a wish! A plan without execution is just that, a plan. It is your actions that make things happen. Think about it. If your life were to be perfect in five years, what would it look like? Write it down and be as specific as you can be with it. Stay clear about what you want, and ask yourself if you're current living or working situation aligns with the goal or desire you wrote?

Stay focused on an endpoint and accept there will be interruptions. Keep the passion going especially when things get difficult or people do not support you. Begin to draw and attract the people, experiences and things that keep you moving forward. What pulls you along the path is the vision you had at the start. *Be focused on the destination but stay flexible on the journey.*

Insight Thirty One, Maintain Personal Resolve

Are you familiar with the *one-percent rule?* Using a *one-percent rule* moves you steadily toward any goal. How do people achieve steady progress? What is their secret? Their secret is they harness consistency, time and focus—*the one-percent rule.*

This rule is a mindset for progress that keeps moving you forward from the start, a little bit each day gets it done even when progress feels slow. You are making daily micro-progress rather than expecting major breakthroughs to materialize.

My writing and producing activities are good examples. It takes me months, if not years, to research, to write, to edit, and then to publish any book—but it is the consistent and persistent commitment (doing a bit each day) that gets it done.

Same with a garden. You plant, water, weed and otherwise tend, and in the end it brings beauty and joy.

I had a client once who had me develop a short term crisis plan for her parents' declining health situation and a longer term, step-by-step action plan to avoid a future crisis. I developed the plan, got her started and she said she was good and would take it from there.

Three years later she called me in another crisis! When I asked about the plan we had developed, she said she moved forward for a couple of weeks and then stopped because the crisis had passed. Now it was a Friday afternoon, and her parents had no home, no money and she expected it all to be magically fixed. It was too late.

Be patient with yourself; change does not happen immediately. If it is important to you it will stand the test of time. Think of one project or aspect of your life that seems overwhelming at this point. Write it down, set a goal and then list three simple steps to move you forward today. *Using the one-percent rule moves you steadily toward a goal.*

Insight Thirty-Two, What's In It For Me

Personal context is the first filter we use in any situation. A common ingredient of any failed change—people advocating for change remain blind to other viewpoints. When confronted with any change, realize most people tune in to their favorite internal radio station, *WIIFM* or *"What's In It For Me?"*

That's not to suggest that people are selfish; it's just that personal context is the first filter we use to evaluate decisions. It's especially true when we're asked to participate in some sort of change.

Ensure that you understand the impact on another person with any change you put forth. Be careful not to inadvertently (or deliberately) filter out information that contradicts your position. Acknowledging and respecting contrary views strengthens your credibility and actually leads to better decisions which lead to better results.

Years ago, I was promoted to a national position and met a person who would now be reporting to me. I enjoyed this person and had great respect for her abilities, so I thought the meeting would go smoothly. I saw a win-win and she saw a win-lose. Why? She wanted the position I was given.

Think about something important to you that involves at least one other person. How determined are you to make something happen? How open are you to let in other viewpoints? *Personal context is the first filter we use to evaluate our own environments.*

Insight Thirty-Three, Break Down The Long View

Are you dealing with a complicated situation? Any overwhelming situation can be managed when the whole is broken down into the sum of its parts. With any important desire or goal, it's best to break down the big idea. If you find yourself embroiled in a situation, it's easy to get caught in discussing the problems rather than deciding on solutions.

Sometimes the temptation to accomplish everything at once creates barriers—barriers that lead to procrastination, paralysis, and feelings of disempowerment. Some people stay focused on the now, unable to visualize the longer term.

When too many people get involved, little gets done. Breaking down an insurmountable situation, helps everyone see the bigger picture and how to contribute. This simple exercise works well in complex situations as I used it for years in my own elder care management practice.

First, determine everyone's commitment; gaining commitment is critical. *Second*, clarify exactly what each person can do and will do; then define each person's ability to take action when there's a problem—set expectations. *Third,* establish realistic schedules; all schedules look good on paper but fall apart in execution because details are forgotten in the planning stage. Things often fall apart when multiple commitments clash. *Fourth,* prioritize problems that are truly urgent and which ones can wait? *An overwhelming situation can be managed when the whole is broken down into the sum of its parts.*

Insight Thirty Four, Plan for Wealth Not Poverty

Do you plan for wealth or plan for poverty? It may seem like a crazy question, but everyday people actually do plan for poverty. For most people, long term planning refers to how you will save and spend your money now and in retirement. Lawyers and financial planners come to mind when you want the greatest return on your investments and from your money. You may want to protect your assets from government overreach.

The greatest problems with this type of preparation is with *long term* ***care** planning.* The cost of *long term care* is catastrophic for many people. Requesting Medicaid planning advice primarily to lessen the economic impact of long-term care is a fool's journey.

But is it "wrong" to protect your assets by engaging in Medicaid planning? The issue of whether Medicaid planning is legal, the short answer is "yes." While it may be legal, is it ethical for lawyers to advise clients—especially those who have accumulated a comfortable amount of assets—to impoverish themselves to take advantage of Medicaid rules intended to help poor people? The short answer is "no."

Originally, Medicaid was established as healthcare for the poor and never designed to cover long term care for anyone and definitely not for people who can afford to pay but hide their assets. The reality is these people who hide money end up with nothing to spend on their own *care needs* and depend upon Medicaid which is drying up in many states. Spend some time in a Medicaid nursing home and ask yourself, "is that a reality I want in my future?"

Whether you have young, dependent children or grandchildren or just planning for your own aging, do you really understand how the healthcare and long term care systems operate? Get advice outside the legal profession before tying up money in various trusts. Be sure you get the full picture before you plan. *Plan for wealth not poverty.*

Insight Thirty-Five, Keep Silent on Your Moves

Do you seek advice from others before deciding for yourself? Do you let in multiple opinions that smother you even though you know what you want?

Whether playing a game of chess, deciding to move to another state or determining the best time to retire, do not announce your moves until you are convinced they are right for you.

Have you ever made a decision that you knew was right and then talked it over with a friend or multiple friends? Then you decided against it even though you knew it was the right decision for you.

Don't let anyone limit your own ambitions—you are not meant to live a life other than your own. Follow your own path, believe in your own dreams and do what your life pulls you to do. *Do not seek advice from others until you are clear on your desires.*

CHAPTER SIX—POWER OF HEALTH

Personal *health* is a personal responsibility that is squarely within your ability to master. Nothing new here. Your state of health results in how you live each day and choices you do or do not make.

On the other side of the same coin is *healthcare*. Healthcare is a transactional service process driven by business methods focused on making money. If you understand these two crucial differences between *health and healthcare*, you are ahead in the game.

Insight Thirty-Six, Health a Verb; Healthcare a Noun

How do you define health? Health as a verb moves you from a state of mind to a state of habit. *Health* is about personal lifestyle and within your ability to control. While genetics play a role, it's your habits and environments that directly influence states of good and poor health.

Health is more than just the absence of disease. Good health requires continued action and awareness. Think about it; something as simple as taking a deep breath reduces your heart rate, increases oxygenation to bloodstream and relaxes the mind. Do you ever consider how many bodily functions happen without your awareness—digestion, breathing, heartbeat, circulation, thinking? Become more aware of them.

Negative emotions harm the body and ongoing negative thinking leads to physical disease. In fact, this negativity not only infects you but contaminates others around you.

Retaining *good health* happens at two distinct levels: individually and within communities. At the *individual level*, daily health practices are the best methods to retain beneficial health. At the *community level*, public health surveillance systems detect threats, such as a food poisoning outbreak, and respond to crises such as pandemics. These public health services are government driven and paid for by federal and state taxes.

Healthcare services are transactional focused on making money. Why? We do not have a healthcare system; we have a disease-oriented system that feeds off illnesses and injuries. While our healthcare systems work well in emergencies and with acute traumas, they fall apart in the day-to-day management of prevention, medical follow up and chronic illness management. The United States healthcare system is unique in this way and consumes almost 20 percent of Gross Domestic Product (GDP) or one-fifth of the economy!

So take a look at your health practices and write down your own "day in my life." What foods do you eat? Drink? How much sleep do you get on a regular basis? Do you exercise and how much of a priority is it in your life? Do you spend time with positive and supportive people in your personal and professional life? Realize that physical exhaustion feels good; emotional exhaustion drains you. *Health as a verb moves you from a state of mind to a state of habit.*

Insight Thirty-Seven, Health Span Equals Lifespan

How long do you want to live? Do you expect to stay healthy until that age? Modern technologies allow us to live longer lives (lifespan), but a longer life doesn't always mean a sustained quality of life (health span)?

Lifespan is how long you are technically alive, and *health span* is the length of time you are healthy and thriving. You want your lifespan to equal your health span. So, if you live to eighty and are healthy until sixty, you have a *lifespan* of eighty years and a *health span* of sixty years.

As we age, we develop chronic illnesses such as diabetes, high blood pressure, or cancers. Many of them can be managed and some reversed or even avoided. In fact, the burden of these illnesses can be *compressed* over a person's lifetime. Wait, what?

Compression of morbidity is a goal for healthy aging and for longevity—living disease-free and illness-free for as long as possible. Morbidity is a medical term that means "suffering a disease or medical condition." *Compression of morbidity* is another medical term that means reducing the length of time a person spends suffering a disease or medical condition.

On a scale of one to ten, how do you rate your general state of health? If you are on the lower scale, do you know why? If on the higher scale, are you aware of your lifestyle habits that contribute to this wellbeing? *Live your life to lengthen your health span to equal your lifespan.*

Insight Thirty-Eight, Avoid the Gaps

Have you experienced breaches when using the healthcare and long term care systems? Do you know what they are and why they exist? Can you identify the *gaps* between short term healthcare and long term care services and how/if insurance covers each one?

Healthcare services are acute, short term, and the most expensive. These services include hospitalizations, physician visits, and some homecare visits. They are transactional, and they are paid by health insurances. These services have a beginning, a middle, and an end point. Insurance coverage is based upon "medical necessity."

Medical necessity describes a person's need for specific types of medical services (such as having a heart attack) in certain care levels (hospital or rehab) and must be justified by a qualified healthcare provider before health insurances pays. If this concept is hard for you to understand, many healthcare professionals also have difficulty understanding it. Yet, this fine line of medical necessity becomes quite visible when the financial shock of unpaid services becomes a reality.

My mother had dementia. When she was hospitalized for pneumonia, her health insurance covered her care. However, once she returned home with ongoing long term care needs, health insurance paid nothing.

Long term care services are just that, chronic and long term. These conditions such as diabetes, heart disease, and dementia develop slowly and do not have an end point. In the United States healthcare insurances do not pay for these types of care needs (which often include bathing, toileting, medication administration, etc.); therefore, the cost of these services is borne largely by individuals and families through private pay dollars or a long term care payer.

Are you aware of the differences between short term and long term health challenges, how they are covered, and their impact on your life? Do you realize of financial implications of each one on your health? *There are huge gaps between short term healthcare and long term care services.*

Insight Thirty-Nine, Healthcare Is a Business

Healthcare services morphed into financial institutions over the past few decades. Instead of operating on sound business plans, they operate on faulty financial plans with the goal of making money at the expense of patient care.

Obscure practices have snuck in such as unbundling the bundles with added fees for healthcare services that appear everywhere. Think of the fast food industry where the cost of a hamburger deluxe finds you paying extra fees for pickles, condiments etc. It happened in the airline industry with fees for baggage and even for leg room. It happens in healthcare when services splinter into various pieces, each with extra fees for so many items. Ever heard of a facility fee? A lab fee?

Where does all that unbundled money go? To the medical industrial complex—to the business of healthcare where money is king. Many providers in this industrial complex are financially self-serving rather than in the business of serving others.

**A significant difference here: There are great physicians, clinicians and providers locked into these toxic systems and is the number one reason for all the worker shortages.*

The Affordable Healthcare Act (ACA) that became law in 2010 is a misnomer as it is not affordable. The ACA provided *access to insurance,* but access to insurance does not guarantee access to affordable care. Why? The goal of insurance companies is to limit care you receive while the goal of medical industrial complexes is to do more to be paid more.

This reality places any patient on a treadmill of three "Rs"—*Recurring* medications someone takes for a lifetime; *Referrals* to specialists who prescribe more medications and *Reductions* in time spent with healthcare physicians and providers to address causes and lifestyle changes. These three practices define modern medicine that drive up costs and leave people in misery. The United States healthcare system spends the most money on healthcare services than any other country and has the worst healthcare outcomes.

If health care providers spent half the time seeking causes rather than just treating symptoms, we would drop the costs of health care and achieve better results. *There's just too much money to be made in disease to focus on health.*

Insight Forty, No Quick Fixes

When you see a healthcare provider, do you want a quick fix or to actually uncover what's wrong? Do you know it's faster and more profitable to give you what you want—a quick fix—than take time to determine a cause? Rather than take time to discuss health issues and options in more detail with patients, many doctors just prescribe medication.

Why? Insurance companies do not pay for tests needed to uncover causes. Providers treat chronic health problems with acute care medical approaches which is an ineffective method. The most effective methods for managing chronic health problems are through lifestyle changes and in finding causes.

Why don't we as patients focus here and demand better treatment? We've been conditioned for the "quick fix," yet quick fixes only manage symptoms—symptoms that are warning signs from your body.

We've become programmed through direct-to-consumer advertising practices. These ads increase the visibility of medications—medications that promote quick fixes. Think about advertisements that continually prod you to "just ask your doctor about the beneficial effects of (*name of medication*)?"

These ads use visuals such as a young woman suffering from severe allergies running through a field of flowers without so much as a sneeze. You are led to believe you can accomplish this feat, but only if you take this medication.

While you relieve symptoms, underlying problems remain. Just think about it. Do you take medication to prevent heartburn so you can eat a greasy, fat-filled meal? If your own biology repels greasy food, it is a sign that the food is not good for your body.

Next time you watch an advertisement for a food or medication, pay attention to the propaganda. Stop numbing internal safety mechanisms with drugs? *It's faster and more profitable to give you what you want—a quick fix—than take time to determine causes.*

Insight Forty-One, Commit to Finding Causes

Treating symptoms, without addressing causes, contributes to poor health and increasing healthcare costs. Too many of us see too many specialists (a whole list of doctors) with no one doctor looking out for your complete health situation (a holistic doctor).

In addressing causes of illnesses, you learn if you lack something the body needs (deficient), or overloaded with something the body doesn't need (toxic)?

Too Little or Not Enough

When your body lacks something it requires to sustain good health, it breaks down and develops disease. Where might you be deficient?

Nutrition. Our food supply provides us with many calories and often little nutrition. We are a nation of overfed and undernourished people. Over the past few decades, foods became more processed with more artificial ingredients added to prolong their shelf lives. As a result, foods we eat lack the proteins, carbohydrates, fats, vitamins and minerals we need to sustain good health.

Decades ago, we ate whole foods without all the processing, we drank clean water and got a certain degree of exercise. Today we live on fast foods, drink artificial products and some of us barely move. No wonder our bodies are breaking down. While vitamin supplements offer some relief, they are not a replacement for healthy eating.

So often we use food when we hurt. This practice can help as long as we remain conscious about food choices. Emotional eaters often inhale food to stuff emotions. This type of eating leads to digestive problems and weight gain.

Sleep. Too many of us exist on activity, little sleep and less time to just relax. Are you the type of person who brags about "how little sleep you need" as a sign of a personal success? Rest and relaxation are just as important to health as food and water.

Social Connections. In this time of online chats and virtual relationships, we lose that face-to-face contact and a sense of belonging. Studies have concluded how strong social and family networks contribute to good health.

Movement and Exercise. Even a little exercise each day improves health dramatically. Doctors agree that if they could put the benefits of daily exercise into a pill, it would cure many ailments.

Too Much or More Than Enough

When your body gets too much of anything, it becomes overloaded which hurts health. Where might you be overloaded?

Pollutants. We live in a polluted world as our bodies continually absorb chemicals. Pesticides we use in our yards and homes; chemicals spewed into the air by industry; and toxic waste dumped into oceans and streams surround us. Our genetics directly influence our ability to tolerate and excrete certain toxins and substances. What may be a mere annoyance to one person (pollen and stuffy nose) can be life threatening to another (severe allergic reaction).

Stress. Stress releases unhealthy amounts of internal chemicals (such as cortisol) that aren't good for the body. While it is impossible to avoid stress, there are many ways to manage it, such as rest, positive social connections and exercise.

Thoughts. Remember what you think about you attract to you. If your thoughts are negative, then that negative energy exists within you and harms the body. This negativity also pulls negative energy toward you. You *can* control how you think.

Substance Use. Cigarettes, drugs and alcohol are known toxins! They offer no benefit to the body.

Certain Foods. Companies list ingredients on packages (ingredients listed first on packages are higher amounts). The more ingredients you see listed on any package; the more chemicals you will find in it. Try to eat real foods and avoid the packaged ones.

Medications. No medication is completely safe. Medications don't fix problems better served with lifestyle changes. Try reducing the number of prescription medications by reviewing them with your physician. *Treating symptoms without addressing causes contributes to poor health and rising healthcare costs.*

Insight Forty-Two, Miranda Rights for Healthcare

Have you ever experienced a "navigational nightmare" when dealing with a complex healthcare problem? With multiple segments and varying rules and regulations, you can see why you need a guide and should be guaranteed a guide before you say or sign anything.

Citizens are guaranteed representation to advocate and navigate the complicated array of judicial services and systems; medical services are equally complex. *We need Miranda right for healthcare.*

Your Mirada Rights for Healthcare: *You have the right to remain healthy. If you give up that right, anything you say or do can cause you physical, emotional, and financial harm. You have the right to a qualified advocate; if you cannot afford an advocate, one will be assigned to you. Do you understand these rights as I've read them to you?*

CHAPTER SEVEN—POWER OF WEALTH

Each of us has fixed ideas about wealth as it means different things to different people. For most of us wealth equates to money, and our relationship with money springs from embedded beliefs systems about what it means to be prosperous.

Insight Forty-Three, Facets of Wealth

How do you define wealth—in counting things money can buy or by counting things money cannot buy? Money alone is a narrow view of what it means to be wealthy. In fact, an abundant life has little to do with possessions; wealth has multiple facets—health, relationships, money and time.

Health as wealth is the glue that binds our lives. Without our health, do other types of wealth matter? Many of us fail to invest in our bodies and minds yet simple changes to our nutrition, sleep and activity levels have positive impacts on our health. Finding a healthcare provider you trust and can partner with is the greatest gift you can give yourself.

Social connections as wealth define how we react within the world and interact with others. Social wealth is defined by our values, who we attract and the experiences they bring. How many people are in your life by choice? Be grateful for the people in your life who are there for you as you are for them.

Finances as wealth is where most of us focus when we hear the term "wealth."

Perhaps you view financial wealth as financial freedom—to do more of the things you like and avoid things you don't like. This type of wealth consists of materialism and an understanding of certain areas such as investing.

Time as wealth is ours to spend how we want, where we want, with whom we want. So many people are cash rich and time poor, yet *time* is what most of us crave. We must realize and embrace the fact that time is finite—it is the one gift we cannot get back. As we age we realize that *time* is our most important asset and gift.

True wealth has many facets and is a state of being. *Money is a narrow view of wealth.*

Insight Forty-Four, Prosperity a Verb; Money a Noun

Do you realize *prosperity* is an active state of consciousness? It's about being grateful for what you have. It's knowing that someone's success does not take away from your own and the prosperity of others is not your business.

Do you see yourself as prosperous; something you believe inwardly and project outwardly? This is not easy to do as many of us have been conditioned from an early age about wealth and prosperity. For example, do you believe you aren't worthy of good things happening to you? Have you had a lot of money and then lost it all? Do you believe if you obtained wealth once, you can do it again? Do you settle for mediocrity or chase what you honestly want? Do you live in poverty consciousness?

It is your mindset that creates cycles of abundance or lack—a perpetual focus on lack only attracts more lack; a perpetual focus on abundance attracts abundance. Learn to appreciate what you have.

Money is a thing and an energy—a material product you exchange for goods and good times. You use money for transactions and the value of that money often depends upon how societies regard its worth.

Take a piece of paper and write down your definition of prosperity and how it is different from money? You will be amazed. *Prosperity is an active state of consciousness.*

Insight Forty-Five, Beliefs About Money

Are you aware of your personal beliefs around money? Money itself isn't the problem, it's your relationship with money that matters. Does money serve you or are you a slave to it? Do you believe that "he who controls money has power?" If you lose a great deal of money, do you lose your identity? Is your value defined by your valuables? Do you seek a handout or a leg up when times get tough? Do you believe that money is infinite or there is only a finite supply?

Since childhood, we internalized beliefs about money and accepted them as true. Do you subscribe to a belief that you can't be rich and be a good person at the same time? Is your self-worth defined by your net worth? So many individuals and businesses base their activity on a Return-On-Investment (ROI) factor. A ROI means that if you spend money, where is the return on that "spend" for you or a company? As Einstein once said, *"not everything that counts can be counted, and not everything that can be counted, counts."*

What are your own limiting beliefs about money? Can you make room for a new, prosperity consciousness, one that is not dependent solely on money?

Through the pandemic, many people challenged their beliefs and realized that wealth isn't defined by money but by relationships and time. *Personal beliefs around money and wealth go deep and are often unconscious.*

Insight Forty Six, Financial Basics

Do you have a realistic money management system? Managing your money can be simple to understand but difficult to execute. I deliberately included this area on financial health as we don't teach the basic tenets of managing money in our educational systems.

I have gone over this basic process with hundreds of adults during various evaluations and long term care planning sessions to help them understand expense, income, debt, subsidy etc. I do not judge, just explain.

Here are the six areas included:

First, what is your budget process? A budget process is a snapshot of money coming in and going out of the household. Write a list of expenses you have each month; which ones are fixed (such as insurance, rent, mortgage); which ones are variable (clothes, food, entertainment). Then make a list of all income streams (work, investments, passive online, rental properties, royalties), anything that brings money into the home. Then add a line item in expenses for emergency costs (car repairs, healthcare costs) that could arise.

The goal is to spend less than you earn or earn more so you can afford what you spend. Do you know how much you spent last week? Review your budget every month, or every week if you need to get this critical building block in place. There are many personal finance apps available.

Second, manage your debt. Do not take on excess debt and decide if items you purchase are things you really need. Eliminate high-interest debt such as credit cards or private student loans. There is a difference between an asset (home) and an expense (car). If you need to borrow money, find a fixed interest rate that does not change over the lifetime of the loan.

Third, save, save, save! Have emergency money in different accounts for emergencies, for college, and for retirement. If you are not interested in retiring, then save for rainy days. None of us saw a pandemic or another war coming, yet these macro events quickly invade our financial security. A medical event or weather emergency creates havoc with our financial order.

Fourth, avoid binging. Habits and activities can spiral into addictions such as gambling, shopping and overspending. I have a neighbor who has packages delivered every day and is unaware of the intense daily spending. Addiction is an unconscious repetitive behavior in which we lose control. Is this binge spending present in your household?

Fifth, use price comparison apps and websites and compare and contrast. Use resources such as Google shopping, amazon camel, prescription Rx, gas buddy, etc.

Sixth, know that price isn't about the cost of a service or item. Many items and services are negotiable, learn to negotiate. *Set up a realistic money management system.*

Insight Forty Seven, Practice Tithing

Do you share your time and/or money to keep prosperity flowing in life? Do you tithe consistently? What is tithing? Tithing is giving away a portion of your earnings or your time. While you may associate religion to this term, it actually references the inflow and outflow of your wealth be it money or time. A universal law cites a free flow of giving to receiving; however, intention is important here.

Recommendations to tithe ten percent of your income may work for some people, but I think giving what feels right and sharing what you can afford works just as well. Just keep the flow going.

Think about then answer these three questions: *Why* do I want to tithe—what areas motivate me? *Who* or what organizations do I wish to support? *How* will I determine the amount to tithe?

Volunteering is another form of tithing. For me I volunteer time and share my musical gifts either in helping people form choirs or in sharing the joys of music. Think of an area where you could volunteer or otherwise donate time and money to others? *Give time and/or money to keep prosperity flowing.*

Insight Forty-Eight, All Eggs in One Basket

Do you have multiple income streams? Jobs for life with a continuous pension at the end are done and so is any form of job security. Today what you know and how much value you contribute matters more than a wall of degrees. Do you take responsibility for your life or depend on the government or someone else to bail you out?

Ensuring multiple sources of income is something I learned in my thirties and have kept it going—various jobs, writing projects, consulting contracts, and teaching assignments. Today it's no longer about any one job but more about multiple streams of income; so if you lose your job you do not lose all your income. The Internet has leveled the playing field for everyone in this area.

In what ways do you improve your value (keep skills current and know the value of those skills)? Years ago I set out to realize a career dream and attempted to embed a model with multiple income streams into a startup company only to come up short. Why? I chose a business model with design flaws that couldn't grow beyond mediocrity. So I cut my losses and moved on to a design that worked.

This reality, referred to as a *Sunk Cost Fallacy* is a term that describes a tendency to follow through on an endeavor when we've invested time, effort, or money whether or not current costs outweigh the benefits. When it's apparent something won't work, it's time to abort.

Do you depend on just one source of income whether working or retired? Ask yourself, if this one income source went away, would I be OK? *Know the importance of multiple income streams.*

Insight Forty-Nine, Fixing Your Income

Have you fixed your income? Do you have income from a work position, through entrepreneurial efforts or via retirement benefits?

Work brings *active income* and is tied to an activity. Investments and certain other "works" provide *passive income* which flow to you without activity. Examples of passive income include rental property income, book royalties, dividends from stocks or distributions from retirement funds.

When you retire, do you switch to a *fixed income*? A fixed income is when you decide to move away from active income to fixed income streams. While some fixed *costs* go down or go away altogether like a mortgage, other *variable* costs such as medical, food, and fuel increases can erase any gains. Stating that you live on a fixed income implies meager funds.

I never understood government retirement policies where society (taxpayers) pay public employees to go on a thirty year vacation. These practices take away from today's needs for education, infrastructure improvements, and local services.

Years ago *more* people paid into retirement funds (pensions, social security, Medicare) and *fewer* people pulled from them. Today it is just the opposite with more people pulling from these funds and fewer people paying into them. We are on an unsustainable trajectory with the number of retired people disproportionate to net producers, and these social safety nets will not hold. What are your views about fixing your income? *When you fix your income, you limit wealth.*

THE THIRD FORCE—CONNECTING

This third section reviews a variety of life connections from your Higher Power to your inner circles to your communities. The question asked here is "who influences you, who do you influence, and how do you choose your connections?" In fact, are you choosing your connections consciously or just associating with people around you?

Our links to others have powerful effects on our health. Romantic partners, family, friends, neighbors, and social connections influence our biology and our well-being. Wide-ranging research suggests that strong social ties link to a longer life. Loneliness and isolation link to poorer health, depression, and increased risks of early death.

This section includes *Chapters Eight through Ten* and examines the power of spiritual and personal relationships. Insights *fifty through sixty-nine* cover areas that examine our faith, our tribes, and our communities.

CHAPTER EIGHT—POWER OF GOD

Since you are reading this section, I assume you're attracted to this type of information and believe in God or another higher power. You recognize you are a spiritual being having a human experience and understand the power of prayer, presence and appreciation.

God's power dwells within every life and is not something you can contain. It is an energy that transcends life and emanates from our internal being. When connected to God, we feel peace and well-being within. Remember, this life is temporary and we're each here with only a spiritual "green card."

Insight Fifty, The One Becomes the Many

Do you believe we are part of one source? This one *source* of divinity becomes the universe we experience as our life. You are not only your body and mind, but exist as a soul having a body/mind experience. In fact, the closer you are to God the smaller the outer world appears. Nothing manifests this reality quicker than a serious illness.

Because we are one spirit we desire unity. Unity forms the soul of any community and fellowship cements the connection. Just as our organs coordinate to create states of health or illness, unity shifts us from competitive self-interest to cooperation with humanity. We witness this reality in times of adversity when people gather to help one another overcome misfortune and help them to move forward. *Simply put, we are all part of one spirit having a variety of personalities and experiences.*

Insight Fifty-One, Faith a Verb; Religion a Noun

Are you aware that faith stems from individual beliefs? Your *faith* is firmly rooted in your beliefs and practices that put you on your knees before God. Faith with prayer is you talking to God; faith in meditation and silence is God talking to you. When you meditate you close your eyes, focus on your breathing, and absorb the presence of God within.

Meditation is a skill you build to gain insight just as musicians practice to play music with ease. The more you connect, the easier it flows. Go wherever the meditation takes you and you'll be amazed what is revealed to you. Meditating clears your mind, aligns *you with you,* and offers the answers you've been seeking.

Religion is an institution that focuses on aspects of life beyond physical being and pushes a need to do something in order to be saved. Religion builds communities of people who share similar beliefs and brings them together in various states of worship. We connect to God through our collective beliefs and form faith communities. While religions differ from one another, they emanate from universal truths that we are all one.

Not all religions are helpful and some exist to generate money only. If a religion preaches anger and violence, it is not about any higher power. *Faith is an individual belief practiced through a variety of religious customs.*

Insight Fifty-Two, All Religions Express Faith

Have you considered that all major religions share a common wisdom and some version of the Golden Rule? The Golden Rule is to treat others how you want to be treated. Whether in the Bible, the Tanakh, the Koran, the Tao or any other written form, they all send the same message—we are one with a dedicated belief in a higher life. As Albert Einstein one said, *"I want to know the mind of God, the rest are details."*

Religion should be a positive experience; any religion that focuses on negativity, anger, and radical divisiveness moves people away from the light of faith. These types of behaviors are not connected to any God. *All religions are different paths to the same God appealing to our desire for unity and togetherness.*

Insight Fifty-Three, Light a Candle

Do you tend to lose hope when walking through dark times? Along this life journey we sometimes step into darkness created by external circumstances or disappointments and losses; at times anyone can feel abandoned by God. Even if you consider yourself a believer, a wretched emptiness can find you and leave you feeling as if you have been cut off from your own life force.

However, it is within this all-consuming space that life starts to make sense to you. It may be hard to understand, but while in this darkness you don't have to "do" anything; it will be "done unto you." Through your life journey, you continually balance who you were with who you are becoming.

So how to keep your faith and hang onto hope as you travel a dark road? At these times it's important to recognize a sense of *redirection*—when things are not working and you've lost your way, it all points to another path.

Hope is a durable, heartfelt and joyful conviction that our lives are governed by a higher plan that transcends our human cognition. Hope is as important as breath and is an energy and a state of being. *A bad life chapter does not mean you need to start over.*

Insight Fifty-Four, Your Own Higher Purpose

Do you live the same story over and over? Can you move on to write a new chapter? Over the past few years and during the pandemic, our busy lives paused and gave us time to reflect. Our worlds came to a historical tipping point—a reset time to begin a new story, create a better life and pursue a different way of living.

Did you find yourself placing a higher premium on character and relationships rather than wealth and fame? Did you gather more things materially or spend time with people who matter? Has your approach to living worked for you or have you changed your life over the past few years?

We are all in a time of rediscovery—who do you want to be? Why? How can you help others? Where do you contribute to create a better world? What brings you joy and inspires you? Be in that space. *Embrace a new life story and you find yourself doing your life differently.*

Insight Fifty-Five, A Dark Night of the Soul

This insight is not about a tough time or single loss or a life transition; it is about a personal transformation. This term, A Dark Night of the Soul, comes from a poem written by St. John of the Cross in the 1500's. The driving force behind this dark journey is what many mystics and religious scholars refer to as "ego death."

This ego death must happen so that your soul can reawaken. In a sense this darkness is a void from which you emerge to a higher, more spiritually aligned consciousness–a new self. You have to die to self so you can truly live. You have to experience great loss so you can gain everything. You have to lose your way so that you can begin to walk your true path. You must abandon yourself to find yourself. You will come back together again, but first you have to fall apart.

The Dark Night of The Soul is equally complicated as it is simplistic; it is experienced as the space between who you were and who you will become. *While everyone experiences darkness, not everyone will experience a Dark Night of the Soul.*

When you abandon your old self, you enter the darkness where the "old you" is stripped away and the "new you" is under construction. It is in that wilderness space where you lack an identity and it can be a scary place. In darkness, you feel as if you are going absolutely insane. Everything you ever thought you knew about life will be called into question. The very building blocks of who you are as a human being tumble and fall. You feel confused, bewildered, angry, desperate, helpless, and hopeless.

But the darkness does give way to the Light, your Dark Night ends and your new life awaits you. It is a rising spirituality within you that brought the darkness in the first place. People who undergo this journey have been searching for answers to bigger questions their entire life and the darkness comes to provide these answers. No logical sense can be made of what happens during this unfolding. *You have to completely let go of your old self to embrace a more enlightened new self.*

Insight Fifty- Six, Learn Acceptance

Are you someone who fights the process of change to the point of exhaustion? Then, bloody and beaten (at least in a metaphorical sense) you collapse in what feels like defeat. But the truth is when you stop fighting or controlling, you allow yourself to be overtaken by something better aligned with who you are.

Everything inside of you will want to fight the transformation. You will try to will it away, push it away or pray it away. But the more you do, the more painful it becomes. It is the irony of ironies. You struggle to gain control (a sense of) and then experience coherence (things fit together). The only way to achieve it is by letting go and accepting.

This reality hit my life after decades of trying to control and battle forces in my career, which I've referred to as climbing *Mount Greed.* After twenty years of the climb, I lost my passion and surrendered; know that surrender is not selling out.

I allowed this surrender to wash over me and released areas of my life that no longer worked for my highest purpose. And it did get better, much better.

That word "surrender" is not about weakness and giving up. It is different from surrendering to the enemy or surrendering to an opponent, indicating defeat. The concept of surrender is one of the most powerful things anyone can do when struggling with a situation. It literally means to "quit fighting" and pushing against the unwanted; allow the wanted to find you. There is peace in surrender; a calm within a storm.

Life experiences you regret and may resent, the ones you want to hide and forget, are the ones God wants you to use to help others. For me, I shifted from trying to change an industry that did not want to change to changing my own approach; I moved away from planting seeds in toxic soil and began fertilizing healthy ground. I grew a different business that blossomed and created something useful. *Release areas in your life that no longer work.*

CHAPTER NINE—POWER OF TRIBE

As humans, we seek the power of a *collective identity* to call our own. Our earliest ancestors banded together to survive, and today we shape our worlds through tribes and connections—tribes and connections that help form our identity.

Your identity forms at the juncture of birthplace and blood forged by shared beliefs around faith, friends, and values. These interactions created our home worlds with routines and rituals that made us similar until we grew into a life we called our own.

As we age, we all need at least one person who can honestly share our struggles and support us through the good and bad times. It is why we continuously seek out tribal connections.

Insight Fifty-Seven, A Collective Identity

Can you define a group in which you share a collective reason for being? When you think of tribe, your thoughts may drift toward family; however, our tribes do change as we grow. Our lives often start as a group of brothers and sisters who share a common family and loyalty. These relationships *are given* to us when younger and *are chosen* as we get older.

Tribes can be broken by divorce, distance, age, and death. As we change tribes through our lifetimes, the need for a tribe never leaves us. Tribes share a direction and a way of being for survival and spring from four key inner longings: a shared reason, a purpose and identity, shared values, and a fierce sense of loyalty.

Each of us longs for that continuing tribal connection consisting of people who know your story and are there for you. However, the more shared past you have in these relationships, the more present you need to be. Otherwise, you may be forced to relive the past repeatedly.

Given the fractured nature of today's families (picture five people sitting in different rooms, each absorbed with his own screen), and given that many adults often live alone, our "need to belong" goes partially or substantially unmet. Therefore, we seem to be continuously on a hunt for our collective groups.

Be aware that collective groups can form into a *collective ego* that includes gangs and cults—a group unconsciously seeking conflict and requiring some type of opposition to define itself, its boundaries and its very identity.

In contrast, conscious groups do not form to define who they are; they come together as enlightened and connected beings—a vortex for consciousness. This identity is real with significant implications for our emotional health and world healing.

Do you know you are the sum of the five people you spend the most time with? In the next few days, do an audit of people in your tribe and become aware of who is influencing you. *We gravitate toward people and groups that share a common identity.*

Insight Fifty-Eight, Choose People Who Choose You

Who are you attracting in your life? Are you surrounded by friends in need or needy friends? Do these people ignore you until they need something? Are they shallow or do they possess more depth?

When surrounded by positive people, you feel good to be in their presence. Do you surround yourself with people who "get you" and support you? It's a great feeling when someone genuinely wants to be with you and to show interest in how your life is going. It's that friend you can tell unwelcome news and she will listen; you tell her good news and she helps you celebrate.

Get the losers and toxic people (people who suck you dry) out of your life and pull in nurturing relations that bring out the best in you. Ask yourself, who am I around and how do I feel when I am around them?

Stop letting people direct your life and break away from them. If unable to totally break away then limit time with them. People who say things behind your back are the very people who find fault in your life instead of fixing their own. *Choose people who support you and you enjoy.*

Insight Fifty-Nine, Can Only Give What Is Within

Do you feel there is something wrong with you that can only be corrected by someone else? So many people marry to fill these missing pieces within, yet no one can give you what you do not possess inside.

You cannot give to others what does not exist within you. If you grew up in a household where your parents did not practice love, you never learned love. If you do not love yourself, you cannot love others. How comfortable are you alone with yourself? This practice is quite insightful as it reveals the level of comfort you have being with you.

Can you spend periods of time enjoying your own company? If you answered no, it may be time to look at where and from whom you are extracting energy. *Be comfortable with some of the empty spaces within you.*

Insight Sixty, How You See Others Exists Within You

Do you see negativity in others whether you know them or not? Do you look for the differences or similarities? Oftentimes we take our own emptiness and project it onto others. The patterns you react to most strongly in others and misperceive as their identity tend to be the same patterns within yourself.

You perceive faults in others as their identity and do so to strengthen your own ego. As you beat up others with your words, you also beat yourself up. You end up doing to others what you thought they were doing to you.

Knowing and living who *you are not* remains the greatest obstacle to knowing who *you are.* As you learn who you are, be around people who reflect you. If you want more love, be love! What you react to in another you strengthen in yourself. Take practical steps to protect yourself from deeply unconscious people by being conscious yourself.

Think of a person who annoys you and then write down exactly why or what is annoying. Then ask yourself how these annoyances you loathe so much exist within you. It is not an easy exercise to complete.

Just before the pandemic hit, I took a *time out* to replenish, renew and rebrand. I looked deeply into myself and wondered why I was attracting conmen and dishonest people into my professional life? When I looked closer, I realized how much I had grown to hate the work I was doing, so of course I attracted the element that represented all I despised. *Treat yourself with love and respect and you will receive the same from others.*

Insight Sixty-One, Legacy Friendships

How many people in your life are you holding onto just because they have been around you for years? Could these people have shifted into legacy friends?

A *legacy friend* is a person you had a strong bond with in your past but the friendship no longer has any "currency" in your life today. Perhaps your paths have taken different directions (for example, friends marry and have children and you pursue a career); your interests drift apart through a choice or a life changes (such as retiring or starting another business), or there is a geographical separation.

Releasing someone in your life is not always a negative thing. Do you have a long term friend and struggle to find common things to talk about? This person may be a legacy friend. Over time some relationships dissolve and others deepen. Sometimes people can jump right back into a friendship after a prolonged period without contact.

But other relationships change and you wonder who to leave behind and who to bring forward? These transitions are normal and healthy on your life journey. *There are times when releasing long term relationships is the best path forward.*

Insight Sixty-Two, People Show You Who They Are

Have you been surprised by certain behaviors in people around you; people you thought you knew well? Maya Angelou's quote, *"when people show you who they are, believe them"* reminds us to pay attention to behaviors someone demonstrates more than who they claim to be. The pandemic showed us aspects of people we thought we knew and then discovered we didn't know them at all.

Over the past few decades, our country has split and divided. While many people have remained centered, many others have been pulled way off course—or maybe they have been off course and we're just noticing. It's difficult to overcome pre-conceived notions of someone we thought we knew.

Decide whether to walk away or limit time. If you catch someone in a lie, your radar should rise up and stay up. If he did it once, he will do it again as it is a part of who he is. Be honest about your relationships. *When people show you who they really are, believe them.*

Insight Sixty-Three, Dump the "Drain Outs"

Who are the people in your life that build you up? Who are the people who knock you down? Humans suffer more at the hands of each other than natural disasters or wars. People who hold you back are not happy for your successes. Do not do permanent things for temporary people—people who disappear as soon as they get from you what they want.

Carlos Castaneda wrote, *"Does this path have a heart? If it does, the path is good; if it doesn't, it is of no use. Both paths lead nowhere; but one has a heart, the other doesn't. One makes for a joyful journey and as long as you follow it you are one with it. The other will make you curse your life. One makes you strong; the other weakens you."*

When people drain you, you become resentful. Resentment is an emotion that leads to a miserable life, and some people make it their life mission waiting for the next thing to react against. Long standing resentments become grievances, and grievances contaminate other areas of life representing baggage of old thought and emotion. Where in your life do you hold resentments?

Do you keep grievances alive with compulsive thinking? Are people in your life resentful and continuously shedding their grievances with everyone and everything? These *psychic vampires* emanate toxicity.

I had a longtime friend over a forty-year timespan who constantly played the victim. For years, this friendship matched up well with my own need to rescue and to save everyone. As I changed my behavior away from my own rescuing, she continued on her same path of playing the victim and the friendship dissolved. When you change, you take the risk of long term relationships going in different directions.

Try this exercise. Take a sheet of paper and divide into three columns. At the top of the first column write *energize*; the second column write *drain*; the third column write *why*. Down the left side write the names of three to five people (family, friends or coworkers) in your life.

Then determine if they energize or drain you; then check the proper column. In the column under "why," write the behaviors that attract or annoy. *If someone drains your energy, let them know or let them go.*

CHAPTER TEN—POWER OF COMMUNITY

Community is different from tribe as it reflects people who surround your life rather than people you choose to be close to you. Community relations can turn into tribal connections, but most often stay as casual relationships no matter how often you see them. Many of us have communities with church groups, work relations and through other activities.

One thing we've all lost over the past few decades is this sense of community. It has been destroyed by conglomerates, capitalism and concern for self.

Insight Sixty-Four, People Who Walk Their Talk

Do you associate with people who promise and then do not deliver? Have you asked yourself why you accept it? I think we're all worn down with so much "fakeness" and with fake people who pretend to be what they are not.

We see this one play out daily in politics which is why so many people stopped listening to politicians. All too often they say one thing and do another—then in the same sentence ask their people to do as they say not as they do. Fake people have wide circles but few intimate or close relationships.

Positive connections flow from people with integrity—people who are who they say they are and who do what they say they will do. These are people who walk their talk and do not make empty promises—they put words into action. It is a version of the everyday phrase "practice what you preach."

The ability to be in a community requires you follow through and to be consistent with who you claim to be. Have you had relationships with people who promise everything, claim they can do anything and deliver nothing? Why are they still in your life? *Associate with people who have credibility and keep their promises.*

Insight Sixty-Five, Select Rather Than Accept

Do you go along to get along? Just dumping the *drain outs* or walking away from the *fake people* isn't enough. You need to *select* people, places and groups that match who you are. While it's important to let in new ideas, learn to select ideas that match your beliefs and values.

Be aware of who and what you call your community. If you have a need for external approval you not only follow crowds, you can get lost in them. So many people march and protest for *a cause* but have no idea why they do it! Do you get caught up in the political rhetoric or a call to join a group—even if that activity doesn't feel right to you?

Are you able to say no or select something else more aligned with who you are? Are you *afraid* to say no? Are you comfortable with your authentic self within groups? I know many people who prefer their own company to large crowds. At times, I am the same way, alone but not lonely. In fact, I love my solitude and am at peace with who I am. The most fascinating relationship you can enjoy is to be one with yourself.

When you realize that someone or a situation no longer works for you, do something about it. How much emotional or financial suffering do you endure before you walk away? Take a brief review of your life and determine who you've chosen and why. *Ensure you are choosing for yourself rather than consenting to the wishes of others.*

Insight Sixty-Six, None of My Business

Do you base how you feel about yourself on what you think others think of you? *"What you think of me is none of my business."* I love this phrase! This book, written by Reverend Terry Cole-Whittaker, dives into ways to shun fear and false beliefs to discover your own inner path—a route to inborn talents and limitless potential! You have a right to happiness, wealth, and success.

Impressions by others don't have any importance unless you choose to give them importance. The thoughts and actions of others cannot harm you unless you let them in. Honestly answer this question, "Do you live by the perception of what others think of you?"

People who do not "get you" will criticize you, so leave them to their own misery. As an outspoken person myself I have many critics. I respond to their assertions with a one or two word phrase, such as "maybe there's some truth there" or "opinions vary." I do not judge them or go down their rabbit holes. Be the lord of your own thoughts as you hold the keys to your own life. *What you think of me is none of my business.*

Insight Sixty-Seven, Be of Service to Others

Do you share your gifts and talents? Every person has something to offer. If there is a natural disaster, a celebration or a relocation, be there for others. Self-confidence comes from servicing another. Do you know we are hardwired for generosity and educated for greed? Do you think Forbes would list the most generous people in the world instead of the wealthiest people? How would that change the world culture?

Time is the greatest gift we can give to each other. When you use your God given abilities to help another, you are *on mission*. How you use your abilities should light you up. The passion is for you and its purpose is for the other.

When I first started out with my business, there were many people and companies I valued that had focus, purpose, and passion. But over time, too many people and businesses jumped into the eldercare space with their focus only on money. This reality drained me, and I started to consider another line of work. I still remember advice I received from a colleague during that time: *"Kathy, so many people have jumped into this space and muddied the waters so no one has any real value anymore."* It was at this time I knew this part of my life was over; I moved on and did not look back.

How do you define your gifts, talents and interests? Every person has something to offer another. *Share your gifts and talents with other people to lift them up.*

Insight Sixty-Eight, Know Your Purpose

Do you have a purpose or a reason to get up each day? People who have meaning and purpose in their lives are happier, feel more in control and get more out of what they do. They also experience less stress, anxiety and depression. Be around the right people and define your reference groups?

In order to find the next thing of interest, be willing to try something that *may not* work out for you. You'll need to keep trying things until you find something—something that says, "Yes, I have to do this!" You may fail a few times, but consider the losses as steppingstones to your destiny. Here is where people in your community can help. Reach out and just talk to people.

Find a way to articulate your purpose into one short statement. Post it somewhere that you'll see it every day. Tell people about it once you are clear and ask for their support. Follow this purpose as if your life depended on it. Surround yourself with people who are excited to see you progress in your journey. *Define your purpose and relentlessly pursue it with others who "get it."*

Insight Sixty-Nine, Your Book of Life

Have you wondered why some people come into your life and then drift away? You were close for a short time, but circumstances eventually led to a fork in the road. It may be someone who helped you through a challenging time, a stranger who became a friend, a work associate who mentored you as you started a new job.

I had a friend who was in my life for a few years after a divorce, he was there for a reason. He helped me through that challenging time and then we each moved on separately without fanfare or drama. Think of someone who you were close to years ago or more recently. How did that person make a difference for you? What was going on in your life at that time? What was the reason that person was in your life? Know that every person brings you a gift.

I had a close circle of friends while in college—a time of tremendous change—they were there for a season. Then there are people I've known for long time with family and close friends. They have been with me through the good, the bad, and the ugly—they are there for a lifetime. *You are the star of your own life book and other people fill supporting roles.*

Insight Seventy, Universal Need to Belong

Do you recognize a deep need to connect? As social animals, we have a "need to belong." We might not experience this need consciously or even be aware that we have it, but nonetheless it resides deep within us. We live it and we love it! Together, united by a common vision, we conquer most obstacles.

Joining a group improves our *happiness* and emotional *resilience*. The benefits that resonate within a group are important aspects to our sense of self. For example, joining a political campaign can give you a strong sense of affinity with people as you pursue a shared passion. *Remember, a single snowflake is easily blown around, but thousands of snowflakes together can stop traffic.*

We receive support from people within groups and experience their support as more valuable and more meaningful. For example, veterans returning from deployments overseas often feel lonely and disconnected from their families because they believe their relatives don't understand the experiences they had during combat. That inner feeling pushes them to connect with other veterans—the support they get from *fellow vets* registers more deeply.

Joining a group of people who share a common interest or purpose can jump start efforts to enhance social connections. Not only do we feel a greater affinity for people with a shared purpose; these groups accept and welcome us. It could be a local church, synagogue, mosque, or other spiritual venue; a way that forges immediate connections to buffer against loneliness.

Think about your own groups whether a book club, a musical band or a work-related association and ask why this group appeals to you? Community experiencing life together requires frequency, commitment and honesty to make a difference. *Activities resonate on a deeper level when members of the same group align with a common purpose.*

THE FOURTH FORCE—ENGAGING

This fourth section explores how you engage with life, with others and within the world in general. The question here is "what lights me up and how do I stay involved in my own life." Know that if you've gotten this far in life, you've made some right choices.

Engaging in life is about connecting and thriving. You can do it from your home, on the road, through work, alone or with a group. Staying engaged throughout life is critical to good health and happiness.

To continue evolving means to continually challenge certain beliefs. Do you hold fast to beliefs even when evidence contradicts or do you adapt as life changes?

This section includes the *Chapters Eleven and Twelve* that explores powers of hardiness and positive aging. Insights *seventy through eight-four* look at our own self-reliance and how to normalize the aging process.

CHAPTER ELEVEN—POWER OF RESILIENCE

Resilient people draw upon inner strength to cope with and recover from life's challenges such as job loss, financial problems, serious illness, relationship struggles, or the death of loved ones. Resilience is our ability to face and overcome difficulties rather than despair or use unhealthy coping strategies.

It's not about doing it all yourself or being financially independent. Developing a resilient and hardy lifestyle is knowing who you are, taking charge of your own life, continuing to help others, letting others help you and letting go of things that weigh you down.

Insight Seventy-One, Do What You Love

Do you enjoy life and what you do each day? We are all good at something or perhaps good at many things. What activities fill you up and make you happy using your natural abilities? It is through these activities your desires flow with persistence and passion.

Persistence is the cornerstone of any worthwhile endeavor as it pushes you through failures and enables you to withstand the journey. Nothing works at first and most people give up before they even try. Staying the course pushes you forward.

Passion drives persistence. If you don't care about it, it is unlikely you will excel. When doing what you love, no one has to motivate you and it's that desire for the best that pushes you forward. It moves you from mediocrity to excellence.

When you enjoy something, it's easy to stay with it and you become one with the activity. To get started, take a blank piece of paper and make a grid with five rows across the top and five rows down the left side. Across the top, list five things *you know you do well* (skills); down the left side, list things *you love to do* (passions).

For example, two things I *do well* is organize projects and write. Two things I *love to do* are to play music and be outdoors. Where these two items intersect on my page are areas I can spend hours—hours that fly by. I love to write outdoors; I loved to organize groups of musicians and arrange music (bands and choirs); see how it works? You can do it with others as they help generate ideas for you and for them.

So now ask yourself, what does the world need and how can I contribute my talents and passions in areas where my skills and passions intersect? You **can** empower the dreams of humanity with the realization of your own [dreams]. *When you align your interests and passions, you are unstoppable.*

Insight Seventy-Two, Be the Change

Can you make the changes needed to change your life and your story? To write a new life chapter is to enter the unknown and let go of the story you've been telling yourself. *"The secret of change is to focus all of your energy not on fighting the old but on building the new."* Socrates

Changing your mindset stops you from going to the default! View yourself as in charge of your life no matter what you do. Do you feel trapped? Are you resentful? Fearful?

Negative emotions create most of your problems and arise in blaming others for your own experiences. Do you have a vision for your life? Have you thought of putting together a vision board? A *vision board* is a collage of images and words representing your wishes or goals and serves as an inspiration and a guide.

Start with a dream list, do not filter it and have fun. Dream big dreams—a back from the future type of thinking. If your life were to be perfect in five years, what would it look like? Begin to attract people places and things that will move you in that direction.

My vision board includes a music studio within a one-level home shared with my husband, a small production and publishing business, surrounded by family and friends. It doesn't matter if any of it exists today. Be in that space and let the timing take care of itself.

Many people who feel trapped in their lives resemble "flies in a jar without a lid." They stay within an emotional jail cell when all they have to do is look up and fly away. Just do it! Which area of your life has to die so another can live? One story line collapses so another can rise. *To write a new chapter, stop rereading the old one.*

Insight Seventy-Three, Sustain Action

Are you disciplined? Applying discipline, building momentum and making changes requires commitment. You water the garden and trim weeds to grow beautiful flowers or nourishing food. For anything important in your life, move the needle at least one percent a day. Life has dreamed a dream for you; align with it.

As a musician, I practice difficult pieces consistently. If you're involved in a complicated situation, break it down to manageable pieces and move it forward a bit each day. If you are a parent, spend time with your children—time just *for* them. If you are starting a business, ask others who have gone before you for advice.

A project I wanted to share with others kept hitting roadblocks. So I took it online and then to social media channels. I had to expand my own technical abilities but more importantly had to believe in my own ability to learn these new skills. Do not confuse inexperience with being unqualified.

For a couple of years, it felt awful as I went from being an expert to a novice. But I was willing to go through that "suck phase" and made it. I learned how to edit, produce and design online and put my energy into a space where people started to listen and to take note. *When you believe you've exhausted all options, you haven't—Thomas Edison.*

Have you truly knocked on every door? Are you pulling on your own expertise and passions? Move away from wishing things were different to doing one small thing today. Stop chasing things that don't matter. *To make any life change requires commitment.*

Insight Seventy-Four, Wounds to Wisdom

How do you respond to adversity? Do you bounce back or break down when things go wrong? The ongoing shocks that continue to plague us (inflation, pandemic, conflicts, wars and death) taint our lives with uncertainty. When we fail, we hurt and sometimes see ourselves as unworthy.

Blaming someone else only keeps you in a problem. There are no justified resentments as resentment only creates anger and despair in you. Failure isn't an end, it's just a step on the journey. When going through hell, keep going. Remember it's not what happens to you but what you do next that matters.

Your most effective ministry comes from deep hurts, and it is the people closest to you that can hurt you the deepest. Experiences and hurts you regret and resent the most may be ones you want to hide. However, these hurts are the ones you can use to help others.

Disclosing internal hurt is why support groups are helpful as people who experienced similar tragedies share their experiences. Groups such as Alcoholics Anonymous (AA) or cancer support groups come together to use their own wounds to help others and in turn help themselves. *Your most effective ministry often comes from your deepest wounds.*

Insight Seventy-Five, Moving Forward After Falling

Does fear of failure or a fear of success hold you back? Know that we are all professional failures. In fact, I've learned to view any failure as more of a reset than a rejection.

Think about one area of your life that is important to you. Is it a large project looming ahead or a difficult conversation that is long overdue? Ask yourself, how can I make it happen or even better, *why* do I want it to happen?

My own steppingstones consist of three "Cs." The first "C" is commitment—commitment to what I want to do; the second "C" is control—I control my own life; the third "C" is challenge—I view any change as a challenge and not a threat. *Remember that life is a series of comebacks.*

Insight Seventy-Six, Freedom Needs Accountability

Do you accept personal accountability to enjoy the freedoms in your life? The pandemic found many people demanding personal freedoms absent any responsibility for the greater good. They wanted guarantees of instant fixes and ongoing rights without any sacrifice. However, every freedom has a corresponding responsibility, and those who genuinely want liberty must accept the personal accountability it entails.

When that responsibility is not met, as a free society, we legislate that responsibility for the good of all. In other words, freedom without responsibility is only chaos. The point here is liberty and responsibility are inseparable.

Personal responsibility gives life meaning. The more responsibility you take on, the more meaning your life has. The higher degree of responsibility you bear, the richer your life will be. *Every freedom has a corresponding responsibility.*

Insight Seventy-Seven, Learning to Let Go

Do you find yourself focusing on the past extinguishing possibilities for the future? Dwelling on things that happened yesterday, things you can no longer change, only tears down what you can build up today. Instead, accept that what has happened is done and in the past. What holds you back? Guilt, Resentment?

Guilt allows the past to influence the future. While we are products of our past we do not need to be prisoners of it. Get rid of the guilt. *Resentment* hurts you more than it does the other person. It's like drinking poison and hoping the other person dies. It is this venom in you that will kill you.

Anxiety can also plague our wellbeing. Many times we think anxiety results from outer circumstances when it arises from our own repetitive thought patterns. What words describe your situation; are you holding onto a belief or a situation that is best let go? One way to get clear is to spend time in nature and bring a journal.

Each one of us has diverse ways of coping with situations. When you release others to be who they are meant to be, you are free to follow your own destiny. Where in your life are you still fighting something that needed to be released long ago? Learn from it and let it go—remember that every exit is an entrance to something else. *Dwelling on events from yesterday only takes away from today.*

CHAPTER TWELVE—POWER OF POSITIVE AGING

Why does our society view its elders as liabilities? *Ageism* refers to stereotypes (how we think), prejudices (how we feel) and discrimination (how we act) towards older people as if they have no value. People who abhor the elderly often possess anxiety and denial about their own aging.

Medical and public health advances have increased longevity, social security benefits protect against poverty, and Medicare guarantees access to healthcare services. We've extended life and vitality but still consider aging as a disease and fight it with anti-aging products and service flogging.

Insight Seventy-Eight, Normalize the Aging Process

Aging refers to the way we move through life from our first breath to our last one. Chronological age is not a driver of physical age; many young people are disabled and many older adults run marathons. Aging itself is a normal process over a lifetime.

This lifelong aging process crosses four age-specific groups: the first age (anticipation), the second age (expansion), the third age (experience), the fourth age (invisible).

Our *first age, or childhood* (birth to about eighteen years), centers around biological development, learning, and survival. Most children and young adults relish this age and *anticipate* growing into their next year. Do your kids correct you when you state their age of nine and they then say, "No, it's nine-and-a-half?"

Our *second age* or *adulthood* (about twenty-two to sixty-five) focuses on family, parenting, working, and contributing to society. These years are busy and active living lessons we gathered during our first age. These are *expansive* times when we find our purpose and reach for the next great achievement.

Our *third age* or *elderhood* defines an evolving stage of life characterized by personal fulfillment (spanning years from our sixties onward). It includes many positive aspects in terms of engaging socially, retaining functional ability, living life, and sharing knowledge and wisdom. In this age we revise how we think of the aging process and focus on what we have gained not lost. People in the third age are applauded for being active, independent, and healthy, and entering this age tends to suppress concerns for *older aspects of elderhood* dominated by fears of dependency.

Our *fourth age* seeps in without notice with a slow decline in function and includes the waning years of elderhood. With the rapid extension of lifespans over the past several decades, the fastest growing age group is eighty-five plus. This group often faces infirmities of living longer with increasing care needs that invoke a lack of choice and agency. It is this aging without agency that opens the *portals to the fourth age*—collective fears about limitations imposed on an undesired and invisible segment of elderhood.

It is the fourth age many people dismiss, deny and delay until its realities arrive. For people in the third and fourth ages, maintaining a sense of control over both health and lifestyle remains critical. *Aging is a normal process not a disease.*

Insight Seventy-Nine, The Shadow Age

At what point are you old? What do you fear most about aging? While we've increased longevity, it creates conflicts for people whose health and levels of disability run counter to expectations. Slogans such as sixty is the new forty portend images of a third age that is socially desirable because it is not old age. It's why the fourth age is feared and condemned in our society.

Society's delusion of *ageless aging* creates tensions between desires and difficulties of growing older with clear markers of old age coming in forms of assistive technologies and increasing care needs. Illness and disability begin to define people, and concerns for safety shift to services and care plans. In my forty plus years in healthcare and eldercare, I've seen tensions between the third and fourth ages play out in two core areas: loss of independence and loss of privacy.

A loss of independence is feared more than death. Think about your own situation for a moment. What if you could no longer drive or plan your day as you would like? This is the same feeling faced by so many elders, especially individuals living alone. Think about a time when you needed to ask for help, and now think about an elder who believes that their need for help will never end.

A loss of privacy makes anyone feel vulnerable as it puts life activities in a fishbowl. We all have quirks and routines we wish to keep private. So, not only is a person angry that they need help and guilty about being a burden, but now feels an intrusion into daily life.

Perhaps if people felt more supported within their communities, with health and social care services geared to the oldest-old, this fourth age would not remain in the shadows and not be so feared. We clearly have more work to do. *People fear loss of independence and privacy more than death.*

Insight Eighty, A Longevity Revolution

Do you know that baby boomers, and generations that will follow, are shifting the aging paradigm? Think about it; we live about eighteen years in childhood and thirty-plus years in elderhood. While we're invested in helping people live longer, we lack the ability to support people living longer lives.

Dr. Robert Butler explores this extension of human life expectancy in his book, *"The Longevity Revolution: The Benefits and Challenges of Living a Long Life."* He stresses the need to re-examine both personal and societal approaches—not treating the aging process as a medical problem but learning to manage the process of growing older.

Unfortunately, current operational structures of today's healthcare and aging businesses prey on older people. So many service providers make promises that fall short on delivery. Older people are viewed as cash cows for so many in this elder service industry, and this reality is a core reason for worker shortages.

However, the boomer generation is resisting these commodity-based and commercially driven care models and demanding more responsive approaches to the aging process.

At the time of this writing, the nursing home industry is obsolete and dying; the assisted living industry is becoming more regulated; traditional homecare models are disappearing through acquisitions or closing shop.

We're moving toward a new balance focused on integrating services into local communities—a balance that retains an elder's independence and ability to move through the fourth age peacefully. *Be selective and do not allow people or companies to prey on you or elderly loved ones.*

Insight Eighty-One, A Longevity Evolution

Will your older years be the same as the generation before you? I think not. The *Longevity Evolution* differs from the *Longevity Revolution.* The Longevity Revolution is about markets and commoditizing aging while the longevity evolution is how we live life while we move through the ages. A linear lifepath is how we once lived; a cyclical lifepath is how we are now living.

The linear lifepath of past generations found people attending school, pursuing a career for life, marrying and raising a family, retiring and then kicking off. As we move through the twenty-first century, we've shifted into a *cyclical lifepath* where we continuously learn new things and remain engaged until the end. People have careers that last longer with more breaks along the way for learning, family needs, and obligations outside the workplace.

This cyclical lifestyle empowers the future with the present in adding years to middle life creating more flexibility in "work" and "retirement." As life spreads out, and not boxed into specific phases, fewer people leave the workforce and careers become more fluid.

You dial up work when other parts of life are less demanding and dial work down at other times; for example, having children or seeking additional education. There is no endpoint and as long as you can, you will! You shift and grow until you die. We witness this cyclical life now underway with the "Great Resignation" and "Quiet Quitting." Both aim to regain time and balance in life.

Consider these facts: Colonel Sanders began the Kentucky Fried Chicken franchise at age sixty-five; Yuichiro Miura reached the summit of Mount Everest at age 80; Nola Ochs was the oldest college graduate at age 95; Rosemary Smith was the oldest person to drive a Formula 1 car at age 79 fulling a lifelong dream.

So fast forward and imagine you are eighty. Take a piece of paper and make list of regrets; not what you did do but what you did not do. Then realize there is still time to do them. *We are evolving from a linear life path to a cyclical one.*

Insight Eighty-Two, Learning a Verb, Education a Noun

Are you open to learning something new? Community classes, online webinars/podcasts, the Internet, books and workshops remain available for anyone who wants to increase knowledge or simply sharpen skills.

Learning is a lifelong activity with a focus on personal development. There is no standardized definition of *lifelong learning;* it refers to learning activities outside of any formal educational forum, such as a school, university or corporate training.

Education results from learning. For decades, *the education train* was the way to better wealth and happiness. People went to college and maybe graduate school. That school of thought has changed. Today, it doesn't matter if you have an MBA or a PhD; it is the value you bring, and problems you solve in the workplace and your communities that matter. While formal education is important, we also gain knowledge from life experiences.

For me, world travel was my greatest teacher, and I will forever be grateful to have experienced multiple countries, various cultures, and different communities before it got all crazy.

Whether ongoing lifelong learning or formal education, acquiring knowledge leads to wisdom. Wisdom is an ability to use knowledge and experience to make sound decisions and sensible judgments. As we age, we share our wisdom to light the paths for others. *Knowledge comes from learning and wisdom gained in living.*

Insight Eighty-Three, Retiring and Expiring

Are you someone who anticipates retirement or dreads it? Traditional notions of retirement have changed in a time when we live longer and face greater economic uncertainty.

Retiring is a concept I never understood. To me it's a point in time where you stop doing what you had been doing and then what? Do you plan to travel, volunteer, spend time with grandchildren, or improve your golf game? According to the US Census Bureau, the over-65 set is now the fastest growing demographic in the workforce.

Or are you energized thinking about your "next act," be it an encore career or a project you've put off during your adult life. Rewards come in terms of additional income and daily fulfillment.

However, there comes a time in everyone's life when it becomes a tangle of losses and an inability to connect to life experiences compatible you as a person. There comes a time when an older person tires from life and considers it complete especially as health and function decline. *Retiring and expiring; how will you do it?*

Insight Eighty-Four, Embrace Forgiveness

Do you regret something in your past that weighs on you? As we age many of us reminisce about the past, and these reveries can generate powerful feelings of sadness, anger and/or betrayal when focusing on pain inflicted by others.

One way to move through painful reactions is through a process of forgiveness. Forgiveness in clinical terms is defined as *"an act of deliberately giving up resentment toward an offender while fostering beneficence and compassion toward that offender."* Remember, just because you forgive does not mean you trust. Forgiving takes a weight off you and lightens your load.

Every act of our lives matters; the deeds of this life form the destiny in the next. *Live your life so at the end you have no regrets.*

INSIGHTS BY CHAPTER

Chapter One: Power of Thoughts

Insight One, Dominant Thoughts: Be aware of your dominant thoughts as they become your life experiences.

Insight Two, Law of Attraction: It's impossible to get what you want when you push against the unwanted.

Insight Three, Words Reflect Emotions: Your words are powerful and reflect your emotional state.

Insight Four, Life is an Echo: If you get experiences you do not enjoy, examine the experiences you give out.

Insight Five, Recurring Life Patterns. An unexamined life will break down, and what you do from that point forward matters.

Insight Six, When Life Doesn't Fit Anymore: When your life isn't working have the courage to make needed changes.

Insight Seven, Run Your Own Race*:* Life is much simpler when you stop explaining yourself to others and just live a life that works for you.

Chapter Two: Power of Beliefs

Insight Eight, Deeply Rooted Beliefs: Long held beliefs form your character and are often unconscious.

Insight Nine, Emotions Reflect Beliefs: Stop trying to change things to feel better; feel better and things around you change.

Insight Ten, Beliefs Become Biology: Your thoughts and beliefs forge relationships with health and illness.

Insight Eleven, Life From the Inside Out: Millions of people can believe in you yet none of it matters if you do not believe in yourself.

Insight Twelve, Life From the Outside In: Your body is not who you are.

Insight Thirteen, Reality of Expectations: Any desire with a corresponding doubt factor goes nowhere.

Insight Fourteen, Practice Gratitude: Happiness arrives when you appreciate what you have.

Chapter Three: Power of Integrity

Insight Fifteen, Positive Brand: Your personal brand is who you are, what you stand for, the values you embrace, and how you express those values.

Insight Sixteen, Live Own Truth: When standing in own truth, there is no need seek validation from others.

Insight Seventeen, Intuition As a Guide: We all have intuition as an internal guide.

Insight Eighteen, Make It Better or Move On: Let go of the mistake and learn the lesson.

Insight Nineteen, Stay the Course: Maturity is living with the tension between the ideal and the real.

Insight Twenty, Go It Alone: Sometimes it's better to be a lonely lion than a popular sheep.

Insight Twenty-One, The "Why" Behind the Action: Know the intention behind everything you say and do.

Chapter Four: Power of Information

Insight Twenty-Two, Be Responsible: You are responsible for the choices you make and the results they bring.

Insight Twenty-Three, Perception Creates Reality: People with same outward experiences do not have the same inner experiences.

Insight Twenty-Four, Information Integrity: Learn to filter factual from fake information.

Insight Twenty-Five, Source The Source: Trace information to its source to ensure it is credible.

Insight Twenty-Six, Tech a Super Spreader: While convenient and accessible, technology easily delivers toxic content.

Insight Twenty-Seven. Barriers to Trust: Our deep rooted beliefs affect how we approach facts.

Insight Twenty-Eight, When in Doubt, Check it Out: Focus more on *how* to learn than *what* to learn.

Chapter Five: Power of Preparation

Insight Twenty-Nine, Chasms of Neglect and Panic: Identify one neglected area in your life and develop a simple plan.

Insight Thirty, Allow for Detours: Be focused on the endpoint but stay flexible on the journey.

Insight Thirty-One, Maintain Personal Resolve: Using the one percent rule moves you steadily toward a goal.

Insight Thirty-Two, What's In It For Me: Personal context is the first filter we use to evaluate our environments.

Insight Thirty-Three, The Long View: Overwhelming situations can be managed when the whole is broken down into the sum of its parts.

Insight Thirty-Four, Plan Wealth Not Poverty: Plan for wealth not poverty.

Insight Thirty-Five, Keep Silent on Your Moves: Do not seek input from others until you are clear on your desires.

Chapter Six: Power of Health

Insight Thirty-Six, Health a Verb, Healthcare a Noun: Health as a verb moves you from a state of mind to a state of habit.

Insight Thirty-Seven, Health Span Equal Lifespan: Live your life to lengthen your health span to equal your lifespan.

Insight Thirty-Eight, Avoid the Gaps: There are huge gaps between short-term healthcare and long-term care services.

Insight Thirty-Nine, Healthcare is a Business: There's just too much money to be made in disease to focus on health.

Insight Forty, No Quick Fixes: It's faster and more profitable to give you what you want—a quick fix—than take time to determine causes.

Insight Forty-One, Find Causes: Treating symptoms without addressing causes contributes to poor health and rising healthcare costs.

Insight Forty Two, We Need Miranda Rights for Healthcare. Yes we do!

Chapter Seven: Power of Wealth

Insight Forty-Three, Facets of Wealth: Money is a narrow view of wealth.

Insight Forty-Four, Prosperity a Verb, Money a Noun: Prosperity is an active state of consciousness.

Insight Forty-Five, Beliefs About Money: Personal beliefs around money and prosperity go deep and are often unconscious.

Insight Forty-Six, Financial Basics: Set up and use a simple and realistic money management system.

Insight Forty-Seven, Practice Tithing: Give time and/or money to keep prosperity flowing.

Insight Forty-Eight, All Eggs in One Basket: Know the importance of multiple income streams.

Insight Forty-Nine, Who Fixed It: When you fix your income, you limit wealth in your life.

Chapter Eight: Power of God

Insight Fifty, One Becomes The Many: Simply put, we are all part of one spirit with a variety of personalities and experiences.

Insight Fifty-One, Faith a Verb, Religion a Noun: Faith is an individual belief practiced through various religious customs.

Insight Fifty-Two, All Religions Express Faith: All religions are different paths to the same God appealing to our desire for unity and togetherness.

Insight Fifty-Three, Light a Candle: A bad life chapter does not mean you need to start over.

Insight Fifty-Four, Your Own Higher Purpose: Embrace a new life story and you do your life differently.

Insight Fifty-Five, The Dark Night of the Soul: Completely let go of your old self to embrace a more enlightened new self.

Insight Fifty-Six, Learn Acceptance: Release areas in your life that no longer work.

Chapter Eight: Power of Tribe

Insight Fifty-Seven, A Collective Identity: We gravitate toward people and groups that share a common identity.

Insight Fifty-Eight, Choose People Who Choose You: Choose people who support you and you enjoy.

Insight Fifty-Nine, Can Only Give What Lies Within: Be comfortable with the empty spaces within.

Insight Sixty, How You See Others Exists Within You: Treat yourself with love and respect and you receive the same from others.

Insight Sixty-One, Legacy Friendships: There are times when releasing long term relationships is the best path forward.

Insight Sixty-Two, People Show You Who They Are: When people show you who they really are, believe them.

Insight Sixty-Three, Dump the Drain Outs: If someone drains your energy, let them know or let them go.

Chapter Ten: Power of Community

Insight Sixty-Four, People Who Walk Their Talk: Associate with people who have credibility and keep their promises.

Insight Sixty-Five, Select Don't Accept: Ensure you are choosing for yourself rather than consenting to the wishes of others.

Insight Sixty-Six, None of My Business: What you think of me is none of my business.

Insight Sixty-Seven, Be of Service to Others: Share your gifts and talents with others to lift them up.

Insight Sixty-Eight, Know Your Purpose: Define your purpose and relentlessly pursue it with people who "get it."

Insight Sixty-Nine, Your Book of Life: You are the star of your own life book and other people provide supporting roles.

Insight Seventy, Universal Need to Belong: Activities resonate on a deep level when a group aligns with a common purpose.

Chapter Eleven: Power of Self Reliance

Insight Seventy-One, Do What You Love: When you align your interests and passions, you are unstoppable.

Insight Seventy-Two, Be the Change: To write a new chapter, stop rereading the old ones.

Insight Seventy-Three, Sustain Action: Any life change requires commitment.

Insight Seventy-Four, Wounds to Wisdom: Your most effective ministry comes from your deepest wounds.

Insight Seventy-Five, Moving Forward after Falling: Remember that life is a series of comebacks.

Insight Seventy-Six, Freedom Requires Accountability: Every freedom has a corresponding responsibility.

Insight Seventy-Seven, Learning to Let Go: Dwelling on events from yesterday takes away from today.

Chapter Twelve: Power of Positive Aging

Insight Seventy-Eight, Normalize Aging: Aging is a normal process not a disease.

Insight Seventy-Nine, The Shadow Age: People fear loss of independence and privacy more than death.

Insight Eighty, A Longevity Revolution: Do not allow people or companies to prey on you.

Insight Eighty-One, A Longevity Evolution: We are evolving from a linear life path to a more cyclical one.

Insight Eighty-Two, Learning a Verb, Education a Noun: Knowledge comes from learning; wisdom from living.

Insight Eighty-Three. Retiring and Expiring: How will you do it?

Insight Eighty-Four, Embrace Forgiveness: Live life so at the end you have no regrets.

About the Author

A few years ago, I stepped off a career train of money-focused approaches and revolving services to chill out, regroup and determine if I would get back on that train. After careful review, I sold my products, referred clients to colleagues, and adapted my life to its next chapter.

Then the pandemic hit creating huge health, economic and political storms—storms that exposed the problems and the plagues of health and aging services for all to see. During that time, I learned that online platforms are stronger than governments, and it's not about new rules to the game—it's a whole new game.

First, I merged my nursing and communication's activities to leverage my clinical and aging knowledge with decades of publishing experience. Next, I launched an online publishing and production business through my YouTube channel and my Amazon publishing pages. In 2022, I published a book about healthcare *(A Breaking Point, A Boomer's Guide to Protecting Health and Navigating Healthcare),* and another book on renewing life, renegotiating purpose, refocusing relationships, and transforming the way we think about the world *(An Awakening, Clear Passage Through Perfect Storms).* Set to publish in 2023, *The Aging Survival Guide* providing facts, solutions, and realities with real life stories.

Finally, I initiated the *Aging Legacy Project,* a service and a workshop to help individuals assemble their family history, preserve memories and capture life stories. It is a way to pass on thoughts, values, knowledge, and desires to loved ones in written form, individually or with groups.

Made in the USA
Middletown, DE
07 October 2022